The WiseWorking Handbook

....

WISE WAYS TO INCREASE
YOUR VALUE AT WORK

The WiseWorking Handbook

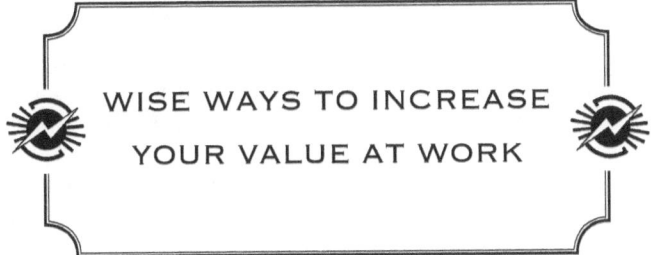

WISE WAYS TO INCREASE YOUR VALUE AT WORK

Craig A. DeLarge

BALBOA
PRESS
A DIVISION OF HAY HOUSE

Copyright © 2014 Craig A. DeLarge.

All rights reserved. No part of this book may be used or reproduced by any means, graphic, electronic, or mechanical, including photocopying, recording, taping or by any information storage retrieval system without the written permission of the publisher except in the case of brief quotations embodied in critical articles and reviews.

Balboa Press books may be ordered through booksellers or by contacting:

Balboa Press
A Division of Hay House
1663 Liberty Drive
Bloomington, IN 47403
www.balboapress.com
1 (877) 407-4847

Because of the dynamic nature of the Internet, any web addresses or links contained in this book may have changed since publication and may no longer be valid. The views expressed in this work are solely those of the author and do not necessarily reflect the views of the publisher, and the publisher hereby disclaims any responsibility for them.

The author of this book does not dispense medical advice or prescribe the use of any technique as a form of treatment for physical, emotional, or medical problems without the advice of a physician, either directly or indirectly. The intent of the author is only to offer information of a general nature to help you in your quest for emotional and spiritual well-being. In the event you use any of the information in this book for yourself, which is your constitutional right, the author and the publisher assume no responsibility for your actions.

Any people depicted in stock imagery provided by Thinkstock are models, and such images are being used for illustrative purposes only. Certain stock imagery © Thinkstock.

Printed in the United States of America.

ISBN: 978-1-4525-6135-6 (sc)
ISBN: 978-1-4525-6136-3 (e)

Library of Congress Control Number: 2012920014

Balboa Press rev. date: 12/16/2014

*To my parents, David and Ethel DeLarge,
and my grandparents, Charles and Grace Brown and Janie Bell Rease
and Robert and Delores McPherson, who first modeled and then
shaped me into the WiseWorker I am today.*

CONTENTS

Introduction xi

PERSPECTIVE:
THE WISEWORKER'S WORLDVIEW 1

1	Practice Improves Everything, So Watch What You Practice	5
2	On a Horse Looking for a Horse	7
3	Opportunity: Who's Pursuing Whom? It or You?	9
4	If I Am Humble, I Cannot Be Overcome	11
5	Everything Comes to Pass	13
6	The Power of "Yet"	15
7	The Progressive Power of "Will Continue"	16
8	It's Not "Either/Or" But "Both/And"	18
9	What Else Will You Do with This Life?	21
10	Work as Worship? Work Is Where I Worship	23
11	Work as Spiritual Retreat?	25
12	Work: Service or Slavery?	26

PERSONAL BRANDING:
THE WISEWORKER'S PERSONA 29

13	You Can't Sell What You Don't Have. Sell What You Have, Not What You Don't!	33
14	Befriending the Impostor (in Ourselves)	35

15	Maintaining Your Sweet Spot in the Midst of Restructuring	38
16	Resume Check, 1, 2, 3...	41
17	Interviews as Value Conversations	44
18	Knowing and Telling Your Value Story	47
19	Deliverables: An Alternative View of Value Presentation	49
20	Enthusiasm: The Dance That Attracts Investment	51
21	Which Is the Better Question: What to Do? or How to Contribute?	53
22	Evil as a Key to Career Satisfaction	55

Networks and Communities: The WiseWorker's Village 59

23	I Love (Organizational) Politics! And You Should Too!	63
24	We Can Make It, But Not Alone!	65
25	Cultivating Customers versus Employers	67
26	Taking the Networking Out of Net Working	69
27	Assuming Innocence: My Relationship Salve and Blood Pressure Reducer?	71
28	The Benefits of Giving the Benefit of the Doubt	73
29	Valuing the Givers More Than the Gifts	75
30	Dealing with the Enemies that Priorities Breed	76
31	Finding (Making) Time for Online Communities	78

Change and Conflict: The WiseWorker's Weather 81

32	Where There Is a Flood, Build a Levee!	85

33	Take It Educationally, Not Personally	87
34	Win the Game You're Playing, Even If You Lose the Games Others Play	88
35	No Problem; Just Change	90
36	Beware of Doing What Makes You Successful	91
37	The Nature of Communication Is Miscommunication	93
38	Patience and Persistence: Two Practices Worth More Than the Effort to Develop Them	95
39	Telling Response-able Stories	98
40	Getting Good at Being in a Bad Mood	99

PRACTICE:
THE WISEWORKER'S PLAYGROUND — **101**

41	No: The New Yes	105
42	Live by Chapters: As for Good Books, So for Good Lives	108
43	Delaying Gratification: Key to Success and Antidote for Procrastination	111
44	Volunteering as a Path to a Better or Different Career	113
45	Eggs, Baskets, and Careers: A Spring Post	115
46	Giving Ourselves (and Others) a Break	117
47	Giving Ourselves (and Others) Credit	119
48	Self-Comparison Better Than Other-Comparison (Most of the Time)	121
49	What Exhausts: The Work or the Reaction to the Work?	123
50	Watching Our Work	125

COMMUNICATIONS TECHNOLOGY:
THE WISEWORKER'S INSTRUMENT AND AMPLIFIER   **127**

51   Facebook: Community Center and Graduate School?   131
52   On Using Delicious Social Bookmarks   134
53   iPhones/iTunes: A Training and Development Tool?   136
54   On Using LinkedIn   138
55   On Using Twitter   141
56   My Unintended Social Media Education Strategy   143

RESULTS:
THE WISEWORKER'S LEGACY   **145**

57   Failing To(ward) Success   149
58   Failure Needs No Plan   151
59   The Pain (and Satisfaction) of Labor   153
60   Wisely Investing Our Own Profit (Margin)   154
61   Time: What Are You Making with Yours?   157
62   Don't Call the Game Before It's Over   159
63   How You Use Your Reasons Determines Whether You Get Results   162

Epilogue   165
About WiseWorking Leadership and Career Coaching   167
Bibliography   169

INTRODUCTION

Welcome to the *WiseWorking Handbook*. This book is the result of insights and experience gained and practiced with successful outcomes during my time as a manager & leader throughout my career. The time when I wrote this book was the most challenging, yet satisfying and developmentally productive period of my career. A few weeks after starting in a new role and quickly detecting the challenge I was in for, I started writing weekly, for thirty minutes, a blog. Over time, these posts accumulated, and here I offer a curated collection of what I believe to be the best among these, organized into categories I have come to refer to as the WiseWorker's Ecosystem, and thus you understand the name of this book, the *WiseWorking Handbook*.

I am one of those people wired to live to work, rather than to just work for a living. I love work. Love professed, I acknowledge that work is hard and difficult and often painful, even when approached wisely, let alone when it is not. In this respect, I am grieved whenever I encounter people who by virtue of a lack of knowledge, wisdom, and good practice are being harmed by their work more than necessary. People spend too many hours of their lives engaging in work for anything less than development, nourishment, and service to be the outcomes. These writings are mindset and attitude we bring to our work, whatever that work happens to be.

After reading through all the writings that make up this collection and giving thought to what I have come to think of as the **WiseWorker's Ecosystem,** I have devised seven categories relevant to wise working.

> **THE WISEWORKER'S ECOSYSTEM:**
>
> **Perspective:** The WiseWorker's Worldview
>
> **Personal Branding:** The WiseWorker's Persona
>
> **Networks and Communities:** The WiseWorker's Village
>
> **Change and Conflict:** The WiseWorker's Weather
>
> **Practice:** The WiseWorker's Playground
>
> **Communications Technology:** The WiseWorker's Instrument and Amplifier
>
> **Results:** The WiseWorker's Legacy

This book has been constructed not so much to be read from cover to cover, though it could be. It has instead been written as a series of quick reads to benefit the reader when in need of quick consolation and encouragement.

Each of these categories constitutes an area that every worker must master on the way to becoming a WiseWorker. If there is one message

INTRODUCTION

I want the reader to take away from this read, it's that approached wisely, work can be a blessed and enjoyable, as well as productive, experience, even in an age of work overload and stress.

I welcome feedback at Craig@WiseWorking.com, subscriptions to my e-mail list at www.WiseWorking.com, likes at my Facebook page, and follows at my Twitter feed, @WiseWorking, as this is only the first of many published works I intend to develop in this area of wise working and I welcome all the advice, direction, and critiques I can get.

PERSPECTIVE

The WiseWorker's Worldview

Perspective: The Wiseworker's Worldview

Because work is difficult, it naturally invites a negative and discouraging perspective. This is why it is important for us to actively maintain a chosen perspective about our work, rather than having it dictated to us by the media, management, colleagues, friends, family, or our own mind, for that matter.

I call this *perspective* the *WiseWorker's Worldview* because our chosen perspective is the underpinning of our experience with work itself.

I can choose to see myself as a victim, or as the master of my experience with my work, as well as my bosses and colleagues. I can see work as a curse or a blessing. I can see work as a necessary evil, or as a means of blessing the world, the society, my community, and my family. Both perspectives are potentially and simultaneously true, but my experience, and that of those around me, depends on which perspective I choose.

In this section, I reflect on insights I have found fruitful in choosing and maintaining my own chosen perspective about work. My favorite, and thus the first, is "Practice Improves Everything," for indeed it does. We then move on to insights varying from valuing the horse we ride to using humility to overcome. In this section, I also feature a collection related to the empowering nature of words like *yet*, *will continue*, and *both/and*, which are worthy of more use in our everyday language. I then take time to reflect on the spiritual nature of work, a perspective that has greatly benefited me.

PERSPECTIVE: THE WISEWORKER'S WORLDVIEW

Practice Improves Everything, So Watch What You Practice

One of my favorite proverbs is "Everything Improves with Practice, so Watch What you Practice." I like to remind myself of this often, especially when faced with the need to develop new skills and ways of thinking. This also applies when I need to avoid the strengthening of counterproductive skills and ways of thinking.

I remember that who and how I am are a function of what I have practiced all my life and that any change will require different practice.

This is particularly relevant at work, as most of my life's practice occurs there. In this practice, I practice patience, knowing that most of my present practices have been in place for twenty years or more, and that change could take just as long, especially when dealing with my thinking, the root of all my actions. In this practice, I fail often, but I also recommit and persist, knowing that flawed practice toward who I want to be is better than perfect practice in being who I do not want to be.

Another relevant proverb is "Every Moment, we Practice Something." This proverb reminds us that whatever we are practicing, we are getting good at it, and will eventually be experts. To this end, we all have to ask what we want to be expert at. Some of us have, through long years of practice, become expert at fear, anger, discouragement, vengeance, procrastination, defensiveness, not taking responsibility, not taking prudent risk, and so on.

We become so expert that we start to think that these characteristics are native to our character and that they cannot be changed. Often, we even become blind to these practices.

Given this tendency in ourselves, we would do well to: 1) become more mindful of who and how we are being, and 2) change our practices in ways that begin to reshape our habit expertise.

Years ago, after doing much damage in my personal and professional relationships, I realized I needed to be more forgiving and less sarcastic, among other things. While not a perfect practitioner of forgiveness and non-sarcasm, I am more so today because of nearly ten years of mindful practice to that end. The same goes for positive thinking, courage, self-encouragement, risk taking, and so on. These are all things I realize I need to become more expert at for my own personal and professional success.

As I have watched my practice over the years, I am happy to say that I have seen the positive result of this practice in my personality, personal relationships, and my impact at work and elsewhere.

This mindful, deliberate practice is difficult and not for the immediately gratified. It is much easier to go through life mindlessly practicing what has been modeled for us by family, friends, professional colleagues, and the media. That said, we should consider that the productivity, peace, and success of ourselves, families, communities, and the world rely upon our practice, for better or for worse.

On a Horse Looking for a Horse

Often in my interactions with clients, I find a disposition of "I have nothing." When I engage them in a "what do you have" discussion, we always find that they have more experience, relationships, knowledge, skill, and education than they acknowledge. This is what I call the "On a Horse Looking for a Horse" mind-set. It is typified by the image of people in the wilderness wishing they had a horse to get them to their destination, all the while discounting the horse they are sitting on. They either fail to acknowledge the horse they have, or they starve that horse and then wonder why it is not taking them anywhere.

Once I came across a quote in my *Zen Page-A-Day Calendar* by John Burroughs. It said, "The lesson which life repeats and constantly enforces is look under foot." You are always nearer the divine and the true sources of your power than you think. The lure of the distant and difficult is deceptive. The great opportunity is where you are. Do not despise your own place and hour. Every place is under the stars, every place of the world."

Inventory, today, the horses you are on that you have not acknowledged or are starving.

- Is it a (work or volunteer) project that you are giving less than your full resourcefulness to?

- Is it a phone book that could be better analyzed and networked with?

- Is it an education that needs enlivening through personal research and study?

- Is it a job role that you should go after, if only to learn what you need to do to qualify for it?

- Is it a 168-hour weekly schedule (which we all have) that neglects your most important priorities in sacrifice to the priorities of others?

- Is it a purpose that you feel (or once felt) in your heart and soul that you have neglected to the damage of your own heart and soul?

- Is it a relationship that is out of sorts, which you know can be set right with a dose of courage, candor, and authenticity?

Whatever horse it is, resolve to cherish and feed it moving forward so that it can get you to where you want to go. Also, remember that there is no better horse than the one you are sitting on and that life is not likely to give you a better horse until you have learned how to ride the one you have. And, of course, if you find you need riding lessons, drop me a note, and we can strategize about that.

Opportunity: Who's Pursuing Whom? It or You?

While doing research for this book on the social network LinkedIn, I came across the question "How do you pursue opportunity?" I was unable to resist answering and added the comment "I believe opportunity pursues me."

As I pondered my reply, it occurred to me that over time I have transitioned from a scarcity mind-set, which dictates that opportunity must be pursued, toward an abundance mind-set, which dictates the opposite.

I believe that opportunity pursues me and my job is to choose which opportunities I will allow to catch me.

The cultivated attitudes of abundance and gratitude have reframed my world in a way that I see opportunity all around me all the time. Opportunities to learn and teach, to serve and graciously receive, to earn and contribute, to live well and responsibly prepare for death, to laugh, and when appropriate, to cry.

To counterpoint, some people might say that they do not have as many opportunities available to them as others, and that would be true. I do not have as many opportunities available to me as some others also. That said, I can do far more with the change in my own pockets than with the billions in Fort Knox, which are not available to me.

My point is that whatever opportunities are available to me, however few, I do better to let them catch and use me for good, than to run from them so they catch someone else instead.

The advice I would give to anyone who thinks he or she has too few opportunities is to let the few opportunities you have catch and prepare you for the larger and greater opportunities you want.

To be more concrete:

- If you want to get a better education, take advantage of the opportunity to expose yourself to the subjects you want to be expert in and connect with people who are better educated in the ways that you aspire to be. (Online courses and social media make this easier than ever.).

- If you want a better occupation, serve and volunteer in ways that allow you to start developing the skills, experience, and contacts that qualify you for that occupation.

- If you want better relationships, commit to training yourself to be a better relater and do the painful, uncomfortable, and frightening work of diversifying the company you keep so you have more instances of good and different relationships over time, as you and the company you keep change over time.

- I could go on, but you see my point. I hope you can begin to understand that opportunity is always pursuing, but we are often too picky or fearful to allow ourselves to be caught.

May we be caught and used by every good opportunity available to us today and every day.

4

If I Am Humble, I Cannot Be Overcome

One of my favorite sayings ever is: "If I am humble, I cannot be overcome."

For a number of years now, this saying has sustained me in situations where I have felt unfairly treated and tempted to be prideful, defensive, and resentful. In those situations, this saying has reminded me that my ability to handle myself well is helped or harmed by the degree of pride or humility I bring to each situation.

Pride tends to cloud my perspective. Humility tends to give clarity. I find that humility is, in effect, an antidote for undue pride and defensiveness.

When I am humble, I am able to, at worst, see the logic in difficult and unfair situations, and at best, see the lesson for my own development in the inflicted unfairness. Humility (not humiliation, by the way) gives me the ability to benefit from the lesson while letting go of the pain the lesson inflicts. It is in this learning and letting go that I overcome (or benefit) in every difficult and unfair situation that life gives me.

Humility has saved me in situations where extreme pride would have destroyed me. I see, on reflection, that humility offered me several advantages, namely:

1. The ability to accept my blind-spots, which were being pointed out by others.

2. The ability to admit to myself, and others, where I was mistaken and needed development.

3. The ability to offer compassion and forgiveness to the fallibility in myself and others.

4. The ability to be grateful, graceful, and hopeful in difficult, complex, and seemingly unfair circumstances.

These advantages have allowed me to gain clarity in confusing situations, to rebuild damaged relationships, to reshape distorted perceptions, and to get derailed endeavors back on track. The more I practice with humility, the more I am convinced that it is a key to many seemingly insurmountable problems and barriers.

This is an invaluable insight as I face more and more seemingly insurmountable problems and barriers, for myself and in others, as a function of my growth as a team member, manager, leader and coach.

Remember, if we are humble, we cannot be overcome!

Everything Comes to Pass

I first heard this interesting double entendre during a Buddhist lecture on impermanence. On further research, I found it is attributable in its entirety to Matthew Flickstein in his book *Journey to the Center*:

"Everything comes to pass; nothing comes to stay."

This saying always struck me funny for its two-part meaning. First, everything comes to pass that is meant for us, and second, everything comes to pass (away) and will not stay forever.

I have pondered this a fair amount lately as it reminds me to enjoy everything I have because one day I will lose it. My position, my possessions, my relationships, my health, and eventually my life will all pass away and be lost to me. This is not something to fret over, but to use as an impetus for cherishing everything, and not taking anything for granted.

Being human, loss is painful to me, particularly when I have lost what I worked to acquire. I am prone to anxiously fret, to take loss personally, and to become conservative and cautious. Clear seeing and remembrance of this proverb remind me that the energy of anxious fretting, taking it personally, and extreme conservatism is better converted to mindful appreciation and conscious enjoyment of everything today, because tomorrow all these things will pass away (and my worrying and fretting will not delay this inevitability).

I find that it is better to welcome and cherish the things that newly come to me (as change) than to mourn too long over those things that pass away, whether they were pleasurable or painful. It is easier to do this if I have truly cherished, savored, and enjoyed what I had when I had it.

If I spent the time of possession despising the responsibility of having it, then I am more regretful when it passes away, because I realize I have lost an opportunity. I will also add that we should not procrastinate in enjoying what has come to us because we never know how long we will have it.

This insight in hand (heart and mind), let's resolve to give up the delusion that everything (or for that matter, anything) comes to stay, and instead set our energy to enjoying everything while we have it and before it is lost to us.

The Power of "Yet"

I have discovered the word *yet* is an inspiring and hopeful word. In my coaching, it is quite common that I hear regretful declarations of projects and tasks not done, people not related to, jobs and promotions not obtained, and so on.

Increasingly when I hear these declarations uttered, I verbally tack on the word *yet* to the statement just made. When I do this, the person making the statement usually blinks in confusion, then recognition, as these three letters instantly transform his or her perception from regret to possibility.

You see, *yet* opens up the back end of any final declaration, transforming its meaning to a non-final possibility. If I say, "I did not succeed in [you fill in the blank]," that can always be changed to, "I did not succeed yet," meaning that I still may. The fact that I still may, reenergizes the possibility that if we persevere, plan, and persist, success is still a possibility.

When tempted to declare an endeavor final, remember that it may *yet* be.

The Progressive Power of "Will Continue"

We have looked at the power of the word *yet* and its ability to keep us working toward those outcomes we desire. Recently, it occurred to me that the words *will continue* are similarly powerful for their ability to reflect the progressive nature of those outcomes we are working toward.

So often in my talks with clients, I hear statements such as, "I have to start ..." in regard to projects or tasks that they need to perform, when in fact, they have already started and what they are really referring to is the need to take the next, not the first, step.

The language of repeated first steps can be demoralizing over time because it robs us of the credit and good feeling of being already on the path. This language comes from a stance of discredit, and I encourage my clients to drop it in exchange for the progressive language of *will continue*. This statement recognizes that though I am not perfect, I am consistent and faithful. I may not have reached my goal, but I *will continue* toward it patiently and persistently until I reach it. This is encouraging and empowering language.

The next time you catch yourself saying, "I have to start ..." or "I never ...," take stock of whether these statements are really true or just reflections of your habit of discrediting and denigrating your past and present progress toward your goals. If they are not true, then reframe that language to "I will continue." Do this no matter how long ago in the past you last took a step along that particular path.

Remember that life is a series of paths we follow and the greater crime is that we do not walk them, not that it usually takes more time and effort than we initially envisioned to walk them.

Now let's continue.

It's Not "Either/Or" But "Both/And"

In my coaching practice I often come across what I call "either/or" thinking, where people see that they have too few, and mutually exclusive, options available to them. Such an approach puts us in a box, overly narrows our sense of realistic possibility, discourages us, and keeps us from our potential.

A good mentor of mine once taught me to practice an alternative to "either/or" thinking, called "both/and" thinking. Such thinking acknowledges many options and considers that most options have the potential to be taken in combination with, or in succession to, other options. This thinking broadens our sense of possibility in the present and future. It also encourages and draws us toward our full potential.

Getting from one way of thinking to the other requires the habit of reframing. A few good examples of reframing to "both/and" thinking that I can readily recall, follow.

Once in a workshop I was asking a young lady about her career aspirations, and she related that she wanted to be an auto mechanic and a writer. She lamented that these aspirations confused her as they were unrelated. She felt torn because she saw them as "either/or". I helped her reframe to understand that they were, in fact, "both/and", as the transportation industry makes huge use of writers, spanning from technical to journalistic to marketing. She was stunned as she had never thought of these as possibilities. This reframe allowed her to see the broader number of possibilities available to her in her areas of passion, auto mechanics and writing.

In another coaching situation, I talked with a communications professional looking to apply her talents in a similar role, though a different organizational setting, within her current industry. Unfortunately her selected value-contribution target was shrinking in size in the economy. She saw that either she would nail a job in her selected value-contribution target or she would be locked out of all desirable options. In our further discussion, we were able to reframe in such a way that we expanded the definition of her target industry in a way she had not previously considered. Breaking out of this industry box brought on a both/and epiphany for her as she understood that she had too narrowly defined her value-contribution target. She left our conversation energized and more hopeful about her career search possibilities.

Personally, I had been plagued for many years of my career with the dilemma of my simultaneous desire for the scale of corporate America and the freedom and nimbleness of entrepreneurship. I used to burn up a lot of unproductive energy performing in one environment while pining away for the other.

I am thankful that I reframed this from "either/or" to "both/and". I have learned to perform as an intrapreneur who helps health-care corporations venture into the use of new media and marketing communications models. This role has been a "both/and" situation for me. I stumbled into it as I have worked, over years, to pursue my passions and continually rediscover my sweet spot within the organizations.

So as you go about your life, watch this tendency to put yourself in an "either/or" box and practice reframing to keep yourself progressively more in a "both/and" frame of mind.

What Else Will You Do with This Life?

Pining away for elsewhere is a constant temptation in life and at work. Getting to elsewhere, that next project phase, team role, or company position, can often be disappointing, as it is usually different in experience than in our dreaming. Enjoying elsewhere is short-lived because hoping and working for it is more fun than possessing it. These realities if not handled skillfully can make work miserable.

Accepting these realities, I work to enjoy and value *here* more than *elsewhere*. Here is yesterday's elsewhere. It is what I wished for yesterday, though it is often not what I expected for today. To better enjoy here, I adopted the mantra "What else would I do with my life?"

This mantra is acknowledgment of the fact that what I am doing here and now is just about the most productive thing I could be doing in the world right now. I trust that life is continually presenting the situation that I can best contribute to and influence now, and that elsewhere is a fantasy, which largely distracts from my best present contribution. When I focus on contributing my best now, it better sets me up for the very elsewhere which often distracts me now. This is a tricky business, as you can hear.

Providing for my family and community, serving my customers and industry, and developing my gifts and network are what my life is consumed with the majority of the time. Whether I embrace and enjoy them as play, or despise and resist them as work, the same question is valid: "If I were not doing this, what else would I be doing with my life?"

You see, without a proper attitude, every "here" can be miserable and every wish for "elsewhere" can be wishful thinking that never satisfies.

Yet if you have a proper attitude, every "here" is good as it is.

This mantra has heartened me when bored, distracted, ungrateful, fearful, angered, wanting to escape, or feeling rejected or unappreciated, all attitudes I am tempted with daily. I have to continually remember that every situation is a good reason to engage and contribute here, as well as a perfect setup for a better elsewhere.

Consider this mantra today and every day, whether here or elsewhere.

10

Work as Sacred Service? Work Is Where I Serve

Recently I listened to the audiobook *Thomas Moore on Meaningful Work*, where he talks about the modern division we have established between work and sacred service. We work all week, but we serve on our respective holy days. He describes how in ancient times, and in many traditional cultures, this division did not exist, and so people approached work with a spirit we usually only bring to sacred service and volunteer activities. With the absence of this sense of the sacred in our work, we see work as disconnected from purpose, as drudgery, something to be tolerated until we can escape on the weekend in the short term, and forever in retirement in the long term. What a waste!

As I reflected on Moore's point regarding the attitude of work as sacred service, I considered that work is the most time-consuming (if not important) means we have for contributing, being of service, indeed loving society. It is also the means by which I come to understand how I am made and gifted, and what outcomes those gifts can produce. This being as it is, I am challenged regarding this false division that I have adopted as a postmodern. As a result, I have recommitted myself to bringing the same joy, gratefulness, equanimity, presence, focus, drive, and perseverance to my job that I am accustomed to bringing to my sacred and volunteer service.

With my commitment to this attitude, I have witnessed a greater level of productivity and stamina, the development of higher-quality solutions, and a heightened level of interpersonal influence in my work. I have benefited and I see daily how this attitude benefits my teams, organizations, and customers.

I encourage us all to work to serve and to serve with our work.

Work as Spiritual Retreat?

While listening to a podcast on *Right Livelihood* by Gil Fronsdal (www.audiodharma.org), I was struck by his characterization of the possibility of seeing work as a monastery where people can develop their spirituality. I have always thought of monasteries as retreats where one goes to escape the world and its temptations, and frankly, work as the opposite environment entirely.

This is why this supposition captured both my attention and imagination. The fact is that work, with all its challenges and annoyances, is a great place to practice patience, concentration, compassion, equanimity, self-control, constructive self-talk, gratitude, and so on. Further, the difficult people at work can be seen as good for extra practice, and you can even learn to appreciate them for the benefit of the extra practice they give you.

You can see how this view of work as a retreat (or monastery) for spiritual practice and development can transform your view and attitude toward work, and even more so if you simultaneously see work as a place of where you (sacredly) serve.

As work is continuously challenging, this perspective is comforting, as I consider that I have not only an experiential and financial, but a spiritual, benefit to be gained on the job.

Work: Service or Slavery?

Work is difficult in part because of its propensity for mind-numbing boredom, overwhelming challenge, and difficult people (chiefly myself). When I see these difficult elements of work as adversaries controlling and besting me, I feel I am an unwilling slave trapped and unable to escape. However, when I see these elements as an opportunity to change and shape the world in beneficial ways, I feel I am a willing servant.

I often, in re-centering, recall that the difference between these two feelings, servant or slave, is in the attitude I bring to work and my willingness to see myself in the situation as an unwilling victim or a willing proactive servant (steward and leader). The latter is encompassed in an approach to management called servant leadership. Read Wikipedia for more details.

When I choose to be a servant leader, the difficulty of work is more bearable and certainly more satisfying, as I am more influential and impactful and able to shape relatively more situations in a way that is consistent with the change I want to see in the world. It is common that in the process of working, we slip automatically into a slave mentality, but the beauty of being able to choose is that we can, with practice, become more automatic at slipping back into a servant-leader mentality. Both are difficult, but one is far more satisfying.

Choose service today!

PERSONAL BRANDING

The WiseWorker's Persona

We all have a persona in the world, that thing that we are (and are not) in people's perception. This persona is what marketers call a brand, a set of valued promises that people trust will be delivered consistently when they use a product or service, or in this context, interact with a person. A part of every brand persona is a story.

That story is what helps people to fit that brand into their life routines, whether the brand be idea, object or person. As workers, we are all brand personas, with a story for each of our families, customers, managers, or colleagues. Each one of these people deal with us on the basis of the valued promises we represent to them and the stories they have internalized about us.

This can make work life both easy and difficult, rewarding and discouraging. As such, the same way we get to choose our perspectives, we also get to shape others' perceptions of our personal brands and to tell our own stories in word and deed. The insights in this section are intended to assist us with this persona-shaping process.

Because so much of our persona and story is rooted in negative and weak stances, I take pains in these insights to refocus us. We do this by selling what we have, befriending our impostor, seeking our sweet spot, rethinking our resumes and interviews, finding our value story and focusing on deliverables, enthusiasm, contribution, and evil—yes, that is right, *evil*. Even evil can be a good contributor to our personas and story. Read on to see what I mean.

You Can't Sell What You Don't Have. Sell What You Have, Not What You Don't!

One of the most common and consistent phenomena I come across when coaching people is their tendency to be more articulate about their deficiencies of qualification, experience, education, relationship, and so on, than about the abundance of qualifications, experience, education, relationship, and so on, they have.

I tell them that "You cannot sell what you do not have." Instead, I encourage them to stop talking about their deficiencies and to reframe, and tell me about their abundance and gifts.

This demand is most always met with false modesty, blank stares, perplexity, and so on. I am patient with this as I have a tendency to do such myself. That said, I discourage it as unproductive and useless in the game of inspiring the confidence in others that yields job and project offers, and ultimately a meaningful career. Instead, I encourage and challenge my clients to identify what they have to offer, rather than what they do not. I then refuse to accept any self-deprecatory or apologetic statements that highlight their deficiencies, rather than their abundance.

Certainly there is a time and a place for talk of deficiencies or areas of development, but not before, or more readily than, the conversation about areas of giftedness and strength. Remember that few others are likely to have more confidence in our gifts than we and that too many are more willing to remember our acclaimed deficiencies, than to guess at our strengths.

Most importantly, remember that *we ourselves are the most influenced audience of our own speech and thoughts,* and as such, we do ourselves the greatest disservice when we continually sell ourselves on what we do not have versus what we do have.

Here I need to invoke one of my favorite quotes: "Watch what you practice, as everything improves with practice."

Be well and sell what you have.

Befriending the Impostor (in Ourselves)

Growth has its uncomfortable aspects, and much growth is avoided because of the stretch beyond our comfort zones. An aspect of this discomfort is what is referred to as the impostor phenomenon (IP). Wikipedia defines the IP as a situation where individuals are unable to internalize their accomplishments regardless of what they have achieved in their work or study or what external proof they may have of their competence. They remain convinced internally that they do not deserve the success they have achieved and are really frauds. They dismiss their success as the result of luck, timing, or otherwise having deceived others into thinking they were more intelligent and competent than they believe to be themselves.

Maximizing our growth, potential, and contribution requires the development of a tolerance for, and the skill to work through, the IP. We need to see the impostor as a transitional friend, not an enemy. This tolerance and skill is needed with every new significant role and level of performance we face in life.

Now that I have time to reflect on my life and career, I can see that I have grappled with this IP when I first went to private school, when I went to college, when I started working in corporate America, when I became a manager, when I married, when I became a father, and even now as I continue to develop into a senior manager, a middle-aged man, and a father of adult children. These have, and are, uncomfortable transitions that have become more comfortable with time, training, practice, and the development of skill.

Every one of these transitions has made me temporarily an impostor as I have had to navigate from one way of seeing myself to another. This is where the saying "Fake it until you make it" has come in real handy.

This phenomenon sets up a tension between the comfortable known and the very uncomfortable unknown, between the mastered and the unmastered. It brings out the worst fears of inadequacy and incompetence in us and requires us to master these fears in order to grow. In each of these cases, it is as though we were immigrants moving to another country where we need to learn new customs, language, thinking, and behavior.

I am convinced that if we are going to grow, we cannot escape IP; we can only work through it.

Working through IP can be difficult and painful, as sometimes we are rejected by those people and institutions that we have developed a prior comfort and affinity with. We can be made to feel like sellouts and traitors, and to some degree we may be, but growth requires such. I think it is important to accept that in life, your growth will often make others, especially those not committed to the same type of growth, uncomfortable, and that discomfort will manifest itself in many dysfunctional ways.

Develop an understanding of, and compassion for, these reactions in yourself and others, but do not let them keep you from your growth. When you have accomplished your goals, those who are really for you will acknowledge their pride in your perseverance, and those who do not, well, they were not for you to begin with and ought to have been shed and left behind.

Successful IP tolerance requires:

- acceptance of the process as normal;
- patient perseverance (sometimes for years) with yourself;
- development of a community to encourage you through this process; and
- any training, formal and informal, you can obtain to help you with your transition.

Here's to our coming to peaceful terms with our impostor!

Maintaining Your Sweet Spot in the Midst of Restructuring

So by now most of us either have been or know someone who has been swept up in *restructuring*, the change going on in the job market where one year you are relevant and needed in a given organization and then suddenly not. Such restructuring does not mean that you are not valuable but that the sweet spot where your value is relevant has shifted. Such a shift happens in the context of an organization, industry, network, problem set, geographic location, and so on.

Wherever the shift occurs for you, the point is that you have to stay nimble and aware so you can migrate your value to the new sweet spot that every restructuring naturally creates.

Too many of us believe our value is in a job, title, or organization, when in fact, our value is more in our education, experience, skills, networks, and knowledge. That value, when matched to a need that organizations and groups of customers have, creates what I refer to as the sweet spot.

I have been getting lots of calls from colleagues lately asking me for insights on how to recapture their sweet spots in the midst of restructuring, and here is what I have given in the way of advice:

1. **Reorganize your resume around skills versus jobs.** We have been taught to organize our resumes by job, but the fact is that skills and results are more critical these days than a mere list of jobs and responsibilities. Job-based resumes make potential employers work too hard to find your value. Organize your resume by the skills in the job description, so you are pinpointing your value against what the employer is specifically looking for. Be sure to include results with as many of those responsibilities as possible. Include your job chronology in a section after your skills and results. This is a very difficult exercise, but it will make your resume stand up and sing, while also preparing you to interview better as you will have your relevant skills and results at the top of your mind.

2. **Look for projects in addition to jobs.** The employed, even temps, get jobs faster than the unemployed. It's an unfair bias, but a bias nonetheless. When restructured, stay employed, even if self-employed. Often when an organization does not have a job for you, they can offer you a project as a contractor. Go for jobs, but do not neglect projects. Until you get a job, they will get you income, keep you in circulation, and put you closer to a job than those who are unemployed.

3. **Identify what you have of value and give it away strategically to those who value it.** This allows potential buyers to try before they buy. Know your gifts, resources, and value. Know who values your gifts and resources. Get good at matching the two. Be a go-giver. By the way, check out the book by the same name, by John David and Bob Burg.

4. **Be relevantly differentiated.** Know your unique value proposition (UVP). You must stand out in the crowd. If you are not differentiated on the basis of your UVP, you are lost in the memory and perception of others. People must know you as a provider of above-average performance in the area of your competence. You must learn to communicate this to those who care or who know those who care. This is called *personal branding* and is a critical skill in any sweetspotting scenario.

5. **Be relevantly ubiquitous.** When you nail down your UVP, be everywhere that UVP is relevant. Meet the other experts. Offer your expertise and service in those relevant communities of practice. Speak at relevant conferences. Write and comment on blogs, books, and videos in the area of your UVP. Engage in online forums where relevant discussions are going on. Do research that adds to the field of knowledge. Develop your thought leadership! Practice the go-giver principle! Remember the greater blessing of giving! As you do this, you will come into the projects and jobs you desire in the area of your UVP.

6. **Cultivate your referral network.** Who you know is important, but who knows you is even more so. Know who in your network knows who, and with which organizations they are associated. Ask for connections and referrals, more than for jobs. People can offer more of the former than the latter.

Here is wishing you the sweetest of sweetspots on your journey!

Resume Check, 1, 2, 3...

I am often asked to review the resumes of family, friends, and acquaintances, and to offer my opinion about how they can be improved. Over the years, my most common advice has been distilled into a set of recommendations. These points of advice are based on the premise that a resume, more than a list of your job history, is a justification of your qualification for a specific role. Given this premise, one is hard-pressed to prepare a good resume without tailoring it to a particular position. This is one of the reasons why I advise people to do research to find the descriptions of jobs they are interested in to use as the basis for their resume.

Following are questions to be checked and answered to improve your resume:

1. Is the experience on your resume organized by the skill sets that match the description of the job you desire? I recommend this format in addition to chronological, to make it easier for the employer to quickly see how your experience matches what they are looking for.

2. Have you expressed your experience with examples of quantifiable achievements reflecting the volume of resources you have managed and the results you have achieved, especially in terms of time and money made or saved, relationships created or developed, people managed or developed, growth or efficiencies impacted, and so on. Results are important because this is what employers are paying for, not just tasks performed.

3. Is your resume easily readable (scannable) with 12-point fonts and selective boldfacing and ruling that make the most important information jump off the page?

4. Are you using online social networks such as LinkedIn? If not, check out, "Chapter 54. On Using LinkedIn," later in this book.

5. When writing your resume, are you customizing it to the particular job you are applying for, or are you using a generic resume? I recommend the former.

6. When preparing your resume, are you, when appropriate, using supplemental appendixes that further summarize relevant experience in easy-to-digest formats? I use appendixes that organize my experience by brands/categories, marketing research tools/methods, publications and presentations I have authored, courses/workshops I have taught, training certifications I have earned, graduate research areas I have pursued, and so on.

7. Have you considered developing a portfolio of your career work, which illustrates key projects you have worked on in a case-study format? Such a portfolio will showcase the process

and results of your work in a written, visual, graphical, animated, audio, or video format that brings your work alive beyond the flat descriptions of your written resume. I have a portfolio of the top projects I have worked on in my career, complete with case-study explanations of the problem tackled, approach taken, and results achieved, as well as a picture of the process or result used. I have found this exhibit very helpful in my own differentiation from other candidates.

Happy resume checking to you!

Interviews as Value Conversations

In my coaching, I witness lots of angst over interviewing. Many see interviewing as an interrogation, being on stage, or being judged—all scenarios that trigger fear and aversion. When I witness this, I try to help people reframe to seeing interviews simply as value conversations, conversations between equals who are expressing and seeking value from one another. As such, when parties in these conversations offer each other maximal value, they can best move to offers and acceptances.

Seeing interviews as value conversations has two advantages: relaxation and the expression of situational value.

Relaxation is critical in many situations, but it is especially so in stressful ones like interviewing. David Allen, author of *Getting Things Done*, says that "Our ability to be productive is directly proportional to our ability to relax." He also says that "Only when our minds are clear and our thoughts are organized can we achieve stress-free productivity."

This applies to interviewing, as relaxation allows one to be more articulate, to think more clearly, and to be more present and engaged—all critical to the articulation of one's value.

I empathize with the fact that interviewing naturally carries a certain degree of performance anxiety. That said, relaxation in the face of this anxiety is a learned skill and one that will improve both your interviewing and employability. There is a direct relationship between relaxation and employability, both in a job and before you get one.

All employment relationships are based on recognition of mutual value offered. All employers hire for value in the form of some contribution that will benefit their organizational objectives. All employees accept employment for some value: an income, development opportunities, organizational affiliation, and so on. Interviews are those conversations where these values are matched up, measured, and either accepted or rejected.

Value increases and decreases relative to the situation. From situation to situation, what is valued, changes. All of us have talents, experiences, knowledge, and relationships that have value; however, our ability to size up a market and organizational situation and to articulate our particular value for a particular situation is almost always the difference between gaining an offer or not.

This is why interviewing is best viewed as a value conversation, or a conversation about the situational value one offers. I offer a few suggestions from my own experience to assist with this:

1. Don't interview; converse.

2. Relax using any number of relaxation techniques that can be learned. My favorites are abdominal breathing and smiling.

3. Inventory the value you have to offer. You can only offer what you have in inventory; you cannot offer what you are not aware you have.

4. Do research to understand what is valued in the industry, organization, and role that you are interviewing for. Use websites, books, industry trade publications, blogs and podcasts, answer markets (Quora and Yahoo Answers), and your network as chief sources of this information.

5. Listen for what the interviewer values. I like to draw this out of the interviewer by asking the question "What did you see in my resume that caused you to invite me to this interview?" You can then construct a whole conversation around the answer to this question.

6. Match what the interviewer values with what you have to offer. Be rehearsed in the confident articulation of examples of your value.

Be patient with yourself, as these are new skills that take time and practice. By the way, practice these value conversations in situations other than when you want a job, and you will be that much better practiced when it is time to go for a job you really want.

As you: 1) rethink from interviews to conversations, 2) learn to relax, and 3) improve your understanding and articulation of your situational value, you will see improvements in your employability, contribution, and general satisfaction with your work, and your life as a by-product.

Valuable interviewing to you!

Knowing and Telling Your Value Story

I often engage my clients in discussions about their value at work. I ask them if they understand the value their respective jobs contribute to the success of their organizations. I am not surprised to see the blank stares. Unfortunately, this is too often the case. Most of us do not give thought to this question day to day, nor are we able to articulate our contributed value to our management, peers, reports, or prospective employers.

I challenge each of them to consider why their organizations should not get rid of them and what would be lost if their jobs (or they) were eliminated.

This is critical!

I explain that every role in an organization must:

1. Generate revenue or savings of time, money, or relationships.

2. Reduce/control costs.

3. Improve effectiveness or efficiency of processes or relationships.

If we do not know and cannot talk about our value in these, or other, terms, we are in trouble in today's organizations.

To avoid this trouble, it is critical that we know our value in all the organizations we are members of and that we are able to tell a compelling story about this value. This makes our present positions more secure, and in the case where we have to go, we are able to better conduct value conversations, which open the door to our next opportunities.

Deliverables: An Alternative View of Value Presentation

While I was at a networking dinner once, a participant talked about the increasing importance of deliverables, deliverables, deliverables when demonstrating our value to present or pending management, clients, or stakeholders. While I know this intuitively, how he said it struck me anew and started me thinking about how this is applied.

In my career, I have migrated across multiple philosophies when it comes to presenting my value. Early on, I emphasized tasks, technical skills, and education; then track record, projects, and results; the latest is management and leadership skills; and I wonder if deliverables is next.

As I ponder this emphasis on deliverables, I see that it has implications for how I can restructure my elevator pitch and resume, as well as how I brand myself in my organization and network.

The chief implication is that I review my career primarily for the outcomes it has produced, with a secondary emphasis on how those outcomes were produced, since this cannot be entirely forgotten.

As I inventory these deliverables, I look for trends and categories among them from:

- a quantitative and a qualitative standpoint, and
- a project/technical and people/team/organizational standpoint.

I look for trends in my paid, as well as my unpaid, work, and in my play as well as my work. The point of this is to enable a confident presentation of those outcomes I am most effortlessly best at producing in the world. All of this insight may not end up on any one of my resumes, but the exercise enables me to better understand and present the value that I can produce, whether it be to present management and stakeholders, or God forbid, post-layoff, to a new management and set of stakeholders.

Enthusiasm: The Dance That Attracts Investment

Enthusiasm is an interesting concept, often overlooked and taken for granted when we think about work and the necessity of gaining investment at work.

Over years of coaching, this concept has come up for me twice in compelling ways.

The first was in a workshop I taught called "Finding Your Natural Gifts", where I used a book "*LifeKeys*" by Kise. In one of its sections, this book considers the fact that enthusiasm is derived from the Greek *en theos*, and suggests the idea that when we are enthusiastic, we are in a dance with God.

The second was in Paulo Coehlo's book *The Alchemist*, when Santiago, while working for the crystal merchant, comes to understand, "There was a language in the world that everyone understood, a language the boy had used throughout the time that he was trying to improve things at the shop. It was the language of enthusiasm, of things accomplished with love and purpose, and as part of a search for something believed in and desired." Ever since reading this book, this quote has become a mantra for me.

Work, among many things, is a process by which we seek investment from others in order to achieve mutually desirable outcomes. Every day my management, my team, my stakeholders, and I seek investments of time, attention, money, support, and so on, in order to simultaneously achieve many organizational, group, and personal outcomes.

As there are an infinite number of investment requests being made of a finite pool of investment resources, it is critical that we show up with every investment-attracting resource we can garner, and enthusiasm is one I think we give short shrift to.

I have witnessed enthusiasm as an investment-decision tiebreaker many times. Being enthusiastic does not require that we break out the pom-poms and cheerleader routines, but it does require that love, purpose, belief, and desire, the language of enthusiasm, is consistently evident in how we show up. When it is evident, people will be more interested in investing their time, attention, support, and so on in those outcomes we seek to bring into the world by way of our work.

Be *en theos* today!

Which Is the Better Question: What to Do, or How to Contribute?

In my coaching, the question I most often encounter is, "What do I want to do?"

It seems to me that this question is rooted in typical boredom and dissatisfaction that can be inherent in work. I think we ask this question because we believe that excitement and satisfaction lie in other work. While I do not doubt this can be the case, my own experiences have caused me to increasingly doubt this.

I have engaged in an ever-broadening circle of activities and endeavors as my career has progressed, and I find I am often tempted with feelings of boredom and dissatisfaction. This recurring theme in my existence has caused me to rethink the question I am asking and my clients are asking.

Asking "What do I want to do?" is an inherently self-centered question that originates from a place of self-satisfaction versus one of contribution and service. It seems to me that asking "How do I want to contribute?" is a better question to ask, if only because it is inherently rooted in an assumption of service and benefiting others.

When I start from this place, I can now match my talents (the "what I am good at and enjoy doing") to a purpose. Performing in such a purposeful space adds a dimension of satisfaction to work that better answers the question of work's purpose. It also makes work more beneficial because:

1. I do the most for the world when I am matching my talent to a deliberate and resonant purpose.

2. I receive the most meaningful reward from my work when I am working for some purpose that is meaningful.

This insight has caused me to start asking my clients (and myself) to reframe this question from "What do I want to do?" to "How do I want to contribute?" or "Who do I want to serve?" or "What do I want to accomplish?"

Starting with these latter questions is a better starting point because once you have answered these questions, the outcome of the answer to the former question is more satisfying.

I am happy to say that I am in a place where my contribution question is presently well answered. While what I want to do is communicate, strategize, learn/teach, and coach, it is satisfying to be able to link those "doing" answers to one of my most important contributions answers. My contribution answers at this time in my life are: "contributing to the creation of better online education experiences for people with various diseases and their treaters," and "contributing to helping people discover a better sense of strategy, purpose, and accomplishment in their careers."

These contribution statements make for great psychological and emotional raincoats on those rainy and stormy days of doubt, boredom, dissatisfaction, and frustration that come with any career (and life, for that matter).

So, think. How do you want to contribute today?

Evil as a Key to Career Satisfaction

The idea for this post came to me while reading Koestenbaum & Block's, Freedom and Accountability At Work. It is a fascinating book about work and its ability to assist us with the existential dilemmas of anxiety, guilt, death, meaning and choice.

The chapter of the book that inspired this post is titled "The Reality of Evil," and it suggests five elements of evil for us to consider:

1. It is unacceptable.

2. It is completely real, ever present, and worthy of respect.

3. To be human is to struggle against it, and we can be successful in doing so.

4. This struggle against evil lends meaning to life and defines who we are.

5. Our approach to evil is freely chosen, and we are fully responsible for this approach (whether we embrace this freedom and responsibility or not).

It further offers a number of categories of evil that we might be concerned about:

- ignorance or lack of understanding;
- ugliness of all types: social, political, emotional, and so on;
- weakness manifest as ineffectiveness, powerlessness, disrespect, or failure;
- alienation manifest as injustice or separateness;
- poverty of all types: economic, personal, national, occupational, and so on; and
- chaos or separation from the Oceanic (a.k.a., God).

The author talks about the fact that certain evils resonate with us and form the basis, though unbeknown to us, for our interests, life tasks, purpose, and destiny. Though I had never thought about this before reading this book chapter, I would agree that there is something to this. The author speaks of the person who becomes a scientist or scholar to struggle against ignorance, and the designer or artist who trained to struggle against ugliness.

I can see on reflection that my own career and service choices are a response to my resonant evils. I coach and teach to struggle against poverty, weakness, and ignorance. I am a healthcare marketing communicator to struggle against ignorance, ugliness, poverty, and weakness. I am a designer to struggle against ugliness and ignorance. Getting clear about these struggles has lent a new level of energy, focus, and drive to what I do every day. What a blessed insight!

I encourage you to consider this same issue for yourself. What evil are you struggling against, in whatever small way, and how can you better struggle with it every day?

If you are not satisfied with your present career state, is it because you need to get more engaged in the struggle against your own resonant evil, or because you need to lend more credence to the struggle you are already engaged in?

I wish you well in your struggle. The world depends on it.

NETWORKS AND COMMUNITIES

The WiseWorker's Village

Networks and Communities: The WiseWorker's Village

The best perspective, use of gifts, and shaping of persona and story means little if you do not have networks and communities that value, can be influenced by, and care to utilize what you have to offer.

Every WiseWorker needs these relational and political resources to effectively produce results. Indeed, every career is built on the advice, insight, support, encouragement, championship, and even opposition of our networks and communities.

Utilizing these resources can be among the most painful and challenging aspects of work. Such utilization also holds the greatest opportunity for personal growth and maturity. It is always daunting to me how much the average person I coach neglects his or her networks and communities, while expecting those networks and communities to be there for him or her when he or she is in need. They do not see the care and feeding of their network as a part of work, though they have little problem seeing that care of family is necessary in order to be cared for by family.

Well, this is definitely a part of WiseWorking!

At the end of the day, it is this work village that largely enables and amplifies (or disables and squelches) what we become and produce in a career.

In this section, we consider the love of politics, how we cannot make it alone, that we need customers, even more than employers, and that it is better to work the net than to network. We ponder innocence and benefit of the doubt, and their use as a blood pressure regulator and tools of resilience. We further ponder the need to value those who contribute to our lives more than what they contribute. Because every community also requires prioritization and prioritization breeds enemies. Finally, we look at the value and benefit of making time for online communities.

I Love (Organizational) Politics! And You Should Too!

I love politics! It's what makes organizations, and ultimately society, run, both for good and evil.

Politics gets a bad rap because of its capricious and selfish use by too many, as well as a lack of political skill and will on the part of too many others. What happens is that the under-political malign politics because they are taken advantage of by the over-political, while discounting the advantages they have in life because of the appropriate use of politics in their favor by even others.

The fact is that politics, or the use of power in relationships, is as neutral as a hammer in the hand of a vandal or a carpenter. When we say we dislike politics, what we might better say is that we dislike how "x" person uses politics. I am always concerned when I hear the well-intentioned say, "I won't play politics," because that statement leaves the field to those who would misuse politics. It is for this reason that we who are under-political should commit to getting skilled so we can counterbalance those who are politically ill-intentioned.

One of the best books I have ever read on (ethical) politics is Brandon and Seldman's, *Survival of the Savvy*. I encourage you to take a look at it, and remember that it's not politics that is bad but the wielder of politics. Remember also that every good thing done in the world is by way of politics, the same as every unfortunate thing. If the world is going to be better, it is going to be so to the degree that we engage, versus abdicate, when it comes to being ethical, politically savvy leaders and influencers.

Effective politicking to you!

We Can Make It, But Not Alone!

Over many years of working and coaching, I have increasingly grown to appreciate the importance of cultivating and participating in networks and communities of interest and practice, both formal and informal.

I am concerned with how often I see such networks and communities underestimated and neglected by those I coach. There is a Bible passage that accentuates this point. Ecclesiastes 4:10 says: "For if they fall, the one will lift up his fellow: but woe to him that is alone when he falleth; for he hath not another to help him up." It's so plain, there is really not much more to be said than that.

In a career, it is important to understand the networks and communities one can cultivate and become a productive contributor. You will notice that I stress *contribution* here, as too often, we are not able to benefit from networks and communities when we are down, because we did not contribute anything to them when we were up.

This is difficult for many people because they lack a sense of what they have to offer and fear being taken advantage of if they should offer. Though everyone has something to offer, knowledge of such value and willingness to get past our fear and ego to offer it, is a challenge with which we must all grapple. I believe that if we view networks and communities as insurance policies (of sorts) and development schools (for sure), we fear less and contribute more. Again, so much is about how we see it.

All along a career path, we need people to refer and vouch for us, to advise and train us, to encourage and push us, to pull us up when we have breakdowns and setbacks.

Such accountability partners are critical to our reaching our potential.

I have achieved so much more in my own career than I had originally conceived because of the networks, communities, and accountability partners I have been a part of and contributed to. I am grateful for this, and I am more willing all the time to give, back and forward, what I have gained.

When we contemplate our giftedness and how we will contribute it in the world, it is important to remember that any gift disconnected from a network and community that needs it will remain relatively undeveloped and fruitless.

As we understand and develop our giftedness, we must commit to contributing it to networks and communities that value it. It is with, and through, such networks that we:

- make contributions;
- receive support and encouragement;
- gain development opportunities; and
- earn compensation, both monetary and nonmonetary.

So I end as I started. We can make it in the world, and in our careers, but not alone.

Cultivating Customers versus Employers

In a session of my "Finding Your Natural Gifts" class, the topic of new workplace paradigms came up. One of the points we discussed was the need to get better at gathering customers versus employers. Most of us were raised on the idea that we need to get a good employer who would pay us well enough. This idea is becoming less relevant as we see a shift toward intermittent versus lifelong employment, where: 1) we are only as secure as our latest project and results, 2) reskilling is necessary on an ongoing basis, and 3) one's network is at least as important as one's employer.

I once worked for a man who told me that I should cultivate customers and clients more than employers, as there is safety in diversity. His point was that if I am fired by one employer I am in a jam, but if I am fired by one of multiple customers, I have other customers to tide me over until I replace the one I lost.

His direct point was that it is better to be a business owner than an employee, or at least to have such an approach to one's career. For those of us who prefer to be employees, there is an indirect point, which is that even with one employer, we need to develop diverse groups of customers within, and beyond, our employer organizations.

The word *customer* derives from "custom," meaning "habit." A customer is someone who frequents a particular supplier to the point of it being a habit. We should ask, "Who is in the habit of coming to us for value?"

We need to constantly assess our value and who values it. Every person who values our value is a customer, whether an individual, group, or organization. When discovering these customers, we need to plan how we can get to know and serve these customers. In getting to know them, we need to design and offer increasingly better solutions that they value, and in exchange for this value offered, we need to derive the incomes of attention, referral, and money, which we all need. It is this cultivation of customers that gives us the diversity that represents security in these turbulent economic times.

Take this to heart and mind and do rethink your stance from employer focus to customer focus.

Taking the Networking Out of Networking

In my coaching, I find networking to be one of the most universally fearsome issues for those looking for work. Most of the fear is inflicted by the fact that they label it networking, rather than other, less-loaded terms such as asking for information/help, contacting people with similar interests, joining a club or community, catching up with family and friends, or volunteering.

I find the other issue that scares many people on this topic is that people are either not clear or confident about what they have to offer that is of value, nor are they clear about who wants that value, whether it be in the form of skills, knowledge, or relationships.

I believe that: 1) reframing what networking really is, as well as 2) clarifying what value one has to offer greatly lowers the risk and fear inherent in the label networking.

Here are some general networking tips that have worked for me over the years:

1. Let all your friends, family, professors, pastor/priest, neighbors, and so on know what type of work/career you are looking for. Ask them to refer you for work in their circles of influence, and especially at their companies, as internal referrals have an

advantage when it comes to hiring. Be a pleasant nag on this point. People usually don't take you seriously the first five times you ask.

2. Join and participate in associations related to the industries you specialize or are interested in.

3. Join LinkedIn and other professional social networking sites and use them for all they are worth. See chapter 54, "On Using LinkedIn," later in this book.

4. Know what you have to offer in the way of relationships, expertise, and so on, and offer it generously to others who need it. People help those who help them. This is the law of reciprocity.

5. Volunteer with organizations working on the problems, for the customers, and in the industries that you are interested in career-wise. This will create natural networking and resume-building opportunities for you.

As you pursue these and other networking practices, you will find that your network will make itself. The point is not to network so much as to work the net of relationships that have been given to you.

Productive networking to you!

Assuming Innocence: My Relationship Salve and Blood Pressure Reducer?

A former boss introduced me to the idea of "assuming innocence." It is another term for "giving the benefit of the doubt." I like it because it calls out for me how much I, and those around me, assume guilt in our relations with others at work. The disposition of assumed guilt or innocence is indeed an indicator of the level of trust in a relationship, and where guilty assumption exists, there is work to do.

I find that in practicing assumed innocence as a default, I:

1. check up to disprove the information that would seem to make one guilty and do not assign guilt until the guilty premise is confirmed.

2. find it easier to approach people in the spirit of goodwill and win-win, which in turn makes it harder for them to be defensive, especially when they (or I, for that matter) are at fault.

3. am less likely to spin off (in my mind and emotions) into any number of negative speculations and conspiracy theories that naturally accompany assumed guilt, yielding the benefits of a clearer mind, a relaxed body, and lower blood pressure for me.

4. am making steady deposits into the emotional bank accounts that underpin high-trust relationships that I need in times of inevitable conflict.

I call assumed innocence my relationship salve because it does what salves do—it heals. It is my blood pressure reducer because indignation over assuming others are guilty is the one thing that raises my blood pressure from moment to moment more than anything else in life. I am sure this attitude will save me dozens of relationships and add days to my life via strong productive relationships and good cardiovascular and mental/emotional health over the rest of my life.

Talk about attitude as medicine!

The Benefits of Giving the Benefit of the Doubt

In any job there comes an end of the honeymoon, where getting things done and reading the culture become more difficult than you thought they would be. The resulting frustration and anger that any high-achieving person experiences when faced with this perception is a temptation to bog down, disengage, bail out, and so on. While I have done this in many past cases, in recent times I have decided against this habit, and instead practiced the first and fifth of Covey's, Habits of Highly Effective People, to be proactive and to seek understanding.

I caught myself weaving stories of malice, incompetence, ego tripping, organizational mismatch, and the like regarding what I had been perceiving, rather than more appropriate stories of change and its struggles. I knew that if I stayed in the former mental and emotional space, I would be setting up myself, my team, and my organization for failure, where success and learning are the only acceptable options. With this realization, I resolved to step up and take the risk of giving the benefit of the doubt, first to the difficulties and then to the strugglers. (The cooperators, collaborators, and other such non-difficults in our lives usually don't need such benefit).

I am happy to say that giving such benefit is paying great dividends of learning, insight, and encouragement, as the engagement and open verbal (and nonverbal) communication that come with such benefit teach much about my own poor assumptions and misperceptions. They also teach about the need for compassion and belief in the idea that everyone is doing the best they can, whether it looks like it to me or not. I continually question when it does not look like it to me, if I am seeing with the right eyes. I am grateful for these new eyes, and I look forward to the new ears and nose I will develop as I, moment by moment, choose to stay open, give the benefit of the doubt, and maintain the posture of a student, versus the less productive vice versa.

Valuing the Givers More Than the Gifts

Every gift comes from a giver. Every giver wants appreciation for the gift he or she gives.

We often err in giving more appreciation to the gift than the giver, whether God, our parents, spouses, children, family, managers, colleagues, and so on. I believe this happens because of the human penchant for the new and the easy. You see, we can get new gifts more readily than new givers, and gifts are easier to relate to than givers. Additionally, the consumer-industrial complex gives us many brands as alternatives to human relationship, and we take this bait too often.

Though gifts are often newer and easier to relate to, it is the givers of gifts who challenge us in relationship, that mature us most. Relationship is a major point of life and the chief vehicle of our personal maturity and growth. This latter point is one of the reasons we often gravitate toward brands as an alternative to deep human relationships.

Understanding this, and its implications for our maturity, we should study to be appreciative of the givers of the gifts in our lives more than the gifts they give, no matter how much grief and pain they may cause us. Such is an opportunity for maturity if we use it the right way.

Dealing with the Enemies that Priorities Breed

Competence creates success. Success creates demand. Demand requires prioritizing.

Prioritizing creates friends and enemies based on how our priorities are prioritized.

There are ways to be at peace with these friends and enemies in the midst of out need to prioritize.

The better we become at being and performing our gifts, the more our being and doing will be demanded by others. Because we are finite, this will require us to prioritize, hopefully proactively. This prioritizing requires saying no in word and deed, and no always carries the risk of creating enemies. This fact scares us, which is one of the reasons so many of us reactively prioritize, creating even worse enemies.

When we proactively say no, even those enemies we create respect us, and very often grow to be our friends if their hearts and minds are in the right place to begin with.

If they are not ... well, my grandmother taught me that the person for whom everyone is a friend has no real friends at all.

All this said, there are ways to be at peace with those enemies that prioritizing breeds, and if not at peace with them, at least at peace with ourselves:

1. Proactively practice the No Formula, described in chapter 41, so that people understand that your prioritizing is about a greater good, not a lesser evil.

2. Don't take others' displeasure so personally. Most people get over it eventually. Read Ruiz's *The Four Agreements* for more insight.

3. Always be open to forgiveness and reconciliation. This is necessary in the times when you fail on #2. It also assumes that eventually most people will get over it and be willing to reconcile.

4. Consider your enemies' point of view. This is not about agreement or capitulation, only about compassion and empathy, the two things that most people want even more than agreement.

I could go on, but these four are difficult enough to execute consistently that we will leave it here for now. As you master these, you will be amazed at how your confidence, respect, and results grow in this area of dealing with the inevitable enemies which priorities breed.

Finding (Making) Time for Online Communities

Any of you who know me know that I am a gregarious person, and that since the inception of online social communities, I have carried my gregariousness online. I am an avid user of LinkedIn, Facebook, Twitter, and Google+.

When I encourage people to use online social communities, I routinely get the reply, "How do you find time for that?"

The fact is that I have made time by reducing time on other relatively less valuable activities.

The fact is that I get a lot of smart work done in online social communities. It occurred to me that my online communities have started to become my surrogate cell phone, magazine, newspaper, book club, classroom and industry conference. I have information and people from all over the world on my computer (and phone) screen teaching (and learning from) me about the topics and issues we find relevant to our professional development and functioning.

We inform and help one another better understand and apply what we are collectively learning. It is not much different than the communities of students, worshipers, professionals, friends, and family that I have used all my life to develop myself and serve. They are just online (more accessible and varied) and self-identified (more helpful), making it easier for me to find more of them and get (or give) what I need faster and even more effectively.

Some common benefits I gain from my online communities are:

- news about industry, technologies, opportunities, people, and so on;

- meeting and staying in touch with people who have mutually relevant experiences and relationships;

- assistance with research to find resources, information on trends, and so on; and

- sharpened perspectives as I engage with others to challenge and educate myself about many relevant topics and issues related to my work and life.

Like with every enjoyable thing in life, I have to be disciplined and practice moderation so I do not go overboard, and yes, I could use these communities more for personal entertainment than for professional edification, but that would be less relevant, right?

So if you need more of the benefits I list above in your professional life, think about building your network and involvement in professionally relevant online communities.

I should disclaim that I have not gotten good at this overnight. I have been building this skill set progressively over a number of years. I also regularly have unproductive relapses and persist in rebounding and improving.

Here is hoping to see you online.

CHANGE AND CONFLICT

The WiseWorker's Weather

Change and Conflict: The WiseWorker's Weather

I like to think of change and conflict as the WiseWorker's weather because these are the hot and cold, mild and blustery, wet and dry environments we play in every day of our careers. They are the stuff that shape and impact our development and results.

Most think of change and conflict as negative and neglect to understand that it's a matter of perspective. The fact is that all the good in the world is a result of change and conflict also. Even a promotion and raise at work are the result of change and conflict.

WiseWorkers learn from all weather, developing and achieving their purposes in both turbulent and pleasant weather. In this section, I hope to reshape your view of change and conflict from a stance of fear and dread, to one of hope and fun.

In this section, we start by considering how high a levee we need to address the floods that foul weather brings, and I want to acknowledge my dear colleague who inspired this insight. (She knows who she is but would kill me if I mentioned her name, so I won't.) While addressing our floods, we speak of taking it educationally, not personally, winning the game we are playing regardless of others' games, and seeing change as, well, change, and not a problem. We warn against maintaining our own successful habits too long. We also ask that you accept the inherent miscommunicative nature of communication, to cultivate patience, persistence and response-able stories and to get good at being in a bad mood.

Where There Is a Flood, Build a Levee!

An abundance of skeptics and detractors, as well as supporters, is part of life. We lose energy, time and relationships in life through our lack of attention to supporters versus skeptics and detractors. We also lose through our lack of skill in learning from, and converting, skeptics and detractors to supporters.

We too often default to feelings of shock, anger, fear, and betrayal when encountering skeptics and detractors. Meanwhile, these encounters are always, I repeat, *always*, opportunities to develop and sharpen ourselves and our execution, regardless of others' intentions.

Remember, no small number of persons can ultimately ruin a career.

When coaching on issues of skeptic and detractor management, I like to use the analogy of levees and floods, where skeptics and detractors bring on floods, and we have to commit to being the levee architects who protect our reputations and objectives from these floods.

Our levees are built of our reputations and kept promises, value propositions and contributions, resources and relationships, as well as those of supporters and champions who are willing to vouch for us to our skeptics and detractors.

Floods are inevitable, and so must our building of levees be to combat them. The higher the flood, so much higher must be the levee. Some would say that the levee cannot be too high. Ideas that have helped me stay focused on levee building versus flood fretting over the years are:

- "Focus on your circle of influence versus your circle of concern," from Covey's *7 Habits of Highly Effective People*.

- "Lead from any chair you find yourself in," from Zander's *The Art of Possibility*.

- "You can only sell what you have, not what you do not have," which you can read about in chapter 13 of this book.

- "Know your value, add value to others, and seek value from others," which you can read about in chapter 18 of this book.

As I have observed this positive focus and practice in myself and others, I have witnessed seemingly hopeless situations, relationships, and projects salvaged and succeeding. So remember, the flood is coming, so keep on building that levee!

Take It Educationally, Not Personally

Work is full of judgments, assessments, and feedback. When these are different from what we expect, it can be hard not to take it personally. One of the responses I have been working on since reading Ruiz's *The Four Agreements* and his admonition not to take it personally is to take it educationally.

What I mean by this is that while I can avoid not taking feedback personally, I should not avoid learning from it.

This shift of perspective allows me to gain benefit from all the feedback I get, however fair, unfair, or painful it might be, whomever it comes from, and whatever situation it is given in. This benefit is rooted in the learned balance of knowing what part of feedback to take and which to leave, knowing which feedback is in my control and which is not, and knowing which feedback fits who I am (and can be) and which does not.

So as we daily are judged, assessed, and given feedback, let's stay committed to resisting defensiveness while embracing the opportunity to learn about ourselves and the situations where we must be productive.

Here's to taking it educationally!

Win the Game You're Playing, Even If You Lose the Games Others Play

Life is a game, and we're all in it from the cradle. We all have to play this game, and the point is to play well. Unfortunately, we spend a disordinate amount of time in life bemoaning this game and being stressed out about the games that others play, while excusing (or denying) the games we play.

Many of the games we play are played unconsciously. A key task of maturity in life is to get conscious about our games. That we play different games with different objectives in relationships, groups, and organizations makes for a lot of stress, tension, and frustration. The question is whether we can improve our performance by staying focused on our games while honoring and even aiding others in their games. This is a tricky balance, but not impossible.

A mentor once told me that everyone is "winning the game they are playing."

The problem is that very often we are not aware of the games we are winning or the effect our winning is having on others. In my own career, as well as in those I have witnessed, I have observed many games. Some of them include a game of being right, pleasing others no matter what, getting credit before anyone else, winning or dying trying, being somebody, avoiding risk and mistakes, fitting in with the crowd, and false modesty. These games are not inherently wrong or bad. They are means to ends that allow us to get along in society and our careers. They only become a problem when they are played in an unbalanced, unconscious, and overly selfish way. It should be our task to assure that we play these games in a balanced, conscious, and appropriately unselfish manner.

A few suggestions that I continually use related to game playing are:

1. Know and be aware of the games that you play and stop playing the games that you don't mean to play. Seek continual feedback from those you trust to gain awareness of the games you play.

2. Accept and even enjoy the games that get played, and when you have to, play patiently, persistently, and with a good attitude, always to learn, if not to win.

3. Choose how you will play the games you play. Be proactive, positive and benevolent. Give up the illusion (and the related stress) that you will be able to escape games, and understand they are useful to achieving important objectives in the world. Since you can't escape, at least not short of the grave, play well.

No Problem; Just Change

In my continuous musings and meditations about the challenges of life, I often recall having once read that a valid view of problems is that they are merely issues that need addressing and that they only become problems when labeled as such.

We know that one person's problem is another person's challenge, another's development, another's opportunity, and so on.

As I think about this, it dawns on me that what we call problems, challenges, development, issues, opportunities, threats, and so on, are all forms of change. When the change is what we want or expect, we call it a blessing. When it is different from what we expect or want, we call it a problem.

I submit that seeing so-called problems as change that we have to choose a response to is a less distressful and more empowering starting point than other alternatives. With this perspective, we can better stay open to change in order to identify and capitalize on the opportunity that is inherent in all change.

To wit, I love to recall the mantra "No problem; just change."

Beware of Doing What Makes You Successful...

I believe that everybody is doing what they believe makes them successful. Over time, we have all learned what makes us successful through a process of trial and error, reward and reprimand. In this way, our being, thinking, and behaving are shaped. The dilemma is that sometimes we are doing what *made* us successful in the past, not what *will make* us successful in the future. That we do what we believe makes us successful even when it no longer does has two fundamental implications:

1. It explains much, often odd and dysfunctional, behavior we display and witness at work. While it may not reveal precise reasons for why we operate as we do, it does provide a consoling explanation that calls for a measure of compassion and empathy in how we deal with ourselves and others. While you may not appreciate people's reasoning or actions, you can hardly blame them for doing what they believe will make them successful. The trick is to be aware of those ways of thinking and acting that we believe make us successful, and to be open to feedback that suggests what new means we need to add that will allow us to be even more successful.

2. It calls continually into question if our present being, thinking and acting are sufficient to make us successful now and in the future. When this implication goes unexamined, we can find ourselves failing today with thinking and actions that were useful only in the past. The trick here is to continually get the feedback and insight we need to understand what's useful and what's obsolete as it relates to our future success.

Though difficult, I encourage us to take these two perspectives to heart and mind when in the heat of work, as it is in this heat that we are most prone to mindlessly fall back on practiced habits whether they are any longer making us successful or not.

The Nature of Communication Is Miscommunication

One of the best insights I have ever received about communication is that the nature of communication is miscommunication. Most communication is misunderstood, even as we assume and others acclaim understanding. I believe this is the underpinning of most frustration and every sort of conflict in life. The problem is that we start from a false assumption that we are completely understood when we communicate.

To add days to my life, I have started to assume that:

1. Most of the time I am misunderstood and will need to communicate multiple times through multiple means and formats before I am completely understood, and even then I will need to check back to make sure that understanding has not faded with time.

2. I must communicate to every one of the five senses as best as possible.

3. I must seek feedback from the audience and hope they tell the truth (as they usually will say they understand even when they

do not, either because they are embarrassed or because they truly believe they do).

4. I must use facts, pictures, stories, and other means to gain understanding.

5. Miscommunication can pretty much be assumed until I see my communication manifest accurately in action.

6. Understanding will take longer than I expect, but I will patiently persevere to stay engaged in communication until I am understood.

7. Understanding is progressive and evolving, versus instantaneous.

My family raised me (and so I raised my children) on the idea that "Said once is enough said." This means that if the communicatees do not get it, shame on them. While this philosophy may work to justify the communicator, it does not make for the most effective action in the world. I deem that, though my parents meant well, this is an idea whose time is past.

We all have to choose how effective we want to be, and much effectiveness starts with how we approach communication. So remember, communication is miscommunication by its nature, and the superior communicator (and communicatee) is the one who accounts for this fact in his or her communications.

Good luck with your reduced miscommunication!

Patience and Persistence: Two Practices Worth More Than the Effort to Develop Them

Patience and persistence are two very necessary skills at work and in life; whose neglect robs us of much of a work's pleasure, learning, and rewards.

Experience has taught me that much of my own grief in life is a function of: 1) my own impatience (with myself and others) and 2) my not persisting, in the forms of procrastinating and giving up.

Being patiently persistent and persistently patient requires the ability to be resilient (to recover), as opposed to wishing that we would never fail and beating ourselves (and others) up when we (they) do fail. Work (and life) is full of adversaries, and thus we need not be our own. We need to understand that impatience and not persisting make us just that.

Below are a number of practices I have used over many years to progressively cultivate patience and persistence:

1. I develop reasonable expectations of myself, a natural extension of studying and knowing myself. (I highly recommend Bolles's "*What Color Is Your Parachute?*" on this topic.)

2. I take care of myself so that I can take care of my commitments.

(I highly recommend Loehr's *"The Power of Full Engagement"* on this topic.)

3. I practice being supple: adaptive, flexible, and open to the possibility of unexpected learning and success in every present moment without undue attachment to the result. (I first encountered this concept in Carlson's *"Don't Sweat the Small Stuff"*.)

4. I see every challenge and issue as an opportunity to gather information to learn and to build relationship.

5. I practice relaxation, especially in the most stressful and problematic of situations. I breathe, I smile, I reframe, I stay open, I seek to understand, I give the benefit of the doubt, and I avoid awfulizing. This practice of relaxation is directly proportionate to our personal productivity if David Allen is right in *"Getting Things Done"*.

6. I practice resilience. I expect, and am not surprised or demoralized by, opposition or (emotional, attitudinal, or psychological) breakdowns; I stay committed to rebounding.

7. I accept mistakes, and even failure, as instrumental to learning. I forgive myself and others for this most human of traits.

8. I assume that all is as it should be. I consciously decide how I will respond in order to effect the next best change.

9. I recall that in battle, the best warriors are relaxed, focused, balanced, open and innovative.

10. I recall it takes ten years to become an expert and twenty to become an overnight success.

11. I recall that patient persistence equals preparation, and we all know what Pasteur said about the prepared mind. If you don't, Google it.

All these practices require tremendous patience and persistence in and of themselves, but their reward is more than worth it. The beauty of this practice is that what you practice is what you improve, and I am happy to say that after years of active practice, I am much improved. I wish the same for you.

Telling Response-able Stories

Challenges are always worse when you are experiencing them than when you are thinking about them at the outset.

Experiences tend to have a honeymoon phase where there is excitement and drive, followed by a demoralizing post-honeymoon phase when reality sets in.

I find that during the post-honeymoon phase, it is critical to watch my (inner) story. Every challenge presents the choice to tell myself (and others) one of several stories, and being human, the default tends to be that of a victim, thus the need to watch my story. Doing this requires a deliberate choice to tell another story related to my ability to be response-able (responsible) to the challenges I am facing, not a victim of those challenges.

I find consistently that the story told, to myself and others, becomes the foundation of my mood, attitude, impact, influence, outlook, and success or failure. The good news is that as I have consistently practiced telling a response-able story over the years, this practice has become more the default. I encourage us all to commit to formulating and consistently telling stories of the response-able, not of the victim, in the face of challenges. The good and bad of it has more to do with that story we tell than with the challenge itself.

Getting Good at Being in a Bad Mood

It has been said that moods are like the weather, one moment sunny and the next rainy, and all completely out of our control. That said, what is always in our control is our response to our moods. So often we, and those we work with, take the opposite view of non-control and do lots of damage to relationships and productivity when in a bad mood.

A mark of emotional intelligence and maturity is that we come to respond graciously to our bad moods, rather than using them as an excuse for being ungracious. This is an especially important point for leaders, as their moods very much affect, and can even become, the weather of the teams or organizations they lead.

Here are a few things that have worked for me as I continue to practice being good at being in a bad mood:

1. Be conscious of and take responsibility for proper response to your moods.

2. Be appropriately transparent about your mood with yourself and others so all know what they are dealing with. This reduces stress. Remember there is a positive correlation between peak performance and lack of (di)stress.

3. Model good mood response for those you lead as a critical development practice, as it will pay dividends for them and those they lead.

4. Be patient with your moods and work to do no harm, as they are always temporary, like weather itself.

So while I may not be able to control my moods, I can, as a Wise-Worker, be aware, communicate, and model well in the face of those moods.

PRACTICE

The WiseWorker's Playground

Practice: The WiseWorker's Playground

One of my favorite quote ever is "Everything improves with practice, so watch what you practice."

This quote emphasizes the critical nature of practice. More importantly, it encourages us to improve in productive ways all the time. Fundamentally, our results, and the satisfaction we receive from them, are a function of how we practice.

So since work is practice, I thought it critical to write about, well, practice, and how the WiseWorker approaches it.

In this section we talk about a number of important practices that are essential to WiseWorking, including:

- saying no,
- chapterized living,
- delaying gratification,
- volunteering,
- spreading eggs and collecting new baskets,
- giving breaks and credits,
- self-, versus other-comparison,
- reaction-fueled exhaustion, and
- watching our work.

We also give some suggestions for how to avoid exhaustion at work. Enjoy!

PRACTICE: THE WISEWORKER'S PLAYGROUND

41

No: The New Yes

A staple topic whenever I teach classes on career management is priorities. I espouse the point that without the ability to consistently set and execute against our priorities, all the self-knowledge we gain regarding our interests, personality, value system, learning style, life narrative, and so on, is moot.

This is the case because we will not be able to effectively use these gifts. Priorities really are where aspiration takes action.

To this end, it's important to understand that prioritizing is impossible without the skillful use of the word *no*.

This word is necessary because saying *yes* to my priorities will always require a corresponding *no* to another's priorities, both those of others and my own.

Prioritizing and saying no in a way that preserves relationships, and at best, gains champions for your priorities, requires skill. Ironically, this skillful use becomes more critical the more we live according to our priorities, simply because when we do this, we become more effective, resulting in more external demands on our time from people who witness our effectiveness.

In my course, I offer the No Formula to help with this most difficult, but necessary, skill. Like chess, this formula takes less than a day to learn but a lifetime to master. The formula consists of three explanations:

1. What I cannot (or will not) do.

2. Why I cannot do it (based on my priorities).

3. The options that exist for giving the requestor what he or she wants (usually another resource or time frame).

As simple as this formula may be in description, it is not easy in performance. It requires courage to value your priorities over others' disappointment.

It requires faith that most people will understand when given a good reason and an alternative option.

It requires clarity regarding one's priorities and the ability to articulate such.

Finally, it requires a relaxed, positive and creative mind capable of formulating alternative options and solutions.

While not perfect at it, I have practiced this formula for many years and have found that I am more balanced, satisfied, respected (though not always liked), and effective (in executing my critical life priorities). Also, my relationships have improved as a result of the courage, clarity, and creativity of this practice.

In the learning, there have been mistakes and misunderstandings, as well as miscommunications and misperceptions, but all those have only been my teacher and sharpened my skill. It is critical to note that the most difficult person to practice this skill with is myself, my harshest critic and worst taskmaster.

As I have gotten better at saying no, I have been able to say yes to more of those priorities that are truly important to me, like finishing graduate school, cultivating my teaching and coaching practice, consistently taking a quarterly vacation to recharge, consistently working out to better my emotional, psychological, and physical fitness, taking time for self-development, and so on. This is the reason why I think of the skillful *no* as the new *yes*!

42

Live by Chapters: As for Good Books, So for Good Lives

One of the great blessings and challenges of living in modern society is the vast number of options we have available to us in terms of education, work, career, and so on.

Today, our blessing of choice is greater than most people have had in the history of the world. The challenge of this blessing is that we must choose.

This challenge of choice causes many to procrastinate or be paralyzed. They make no choice for fear that any choice might be the wrong one. The good news is that life is long enough to make many poor choices and benefit from them in time. Another piece of good news is that many choices look poor in the short term, but based on how we handle them, turn out to be beneficial.

I used to believe that going into the pharmaceutical industry (for economic reasons) versus the fashion/design industries (my original passion) was a mistake. Years later, it is clear to me that it was not a mistake, and I have even been able to combine the two in my role as health-care marketer.

I used to wonder if getting married and having children in my early twenties was a mistake, but again, more than twenty years later with a strong, hard-won marriage and two adult children, I see that it was not. I think you see that the difference is in how I have learned to look at these situations.

My ability to cultivate this view derives from the concept of chaptering, which is based on the fact that life happens in chapters, or stages.

As such, we are always moving through one chapter toward the next. Psalms 90:9b says that "We spend our years as a tale that is told."

Like a good book, life does happen in chapters. As in books, chapters give life a sense of order, structure and continuity. Any present situation (chapter), however difficult, is always in the process of passing by to the next chapter. No chapter lasts forever. With this in mind, I have learned to better enjoy my present circumstances, as I know that they will not last, and that when they are past, I will probably long for some aspect of what is past. I fret less over what I am not able to do today, knowing that there will be opportunities in a later chapter of life to do what I cannot today. Knowing this, I spend time in my present performance planning and preparing for later chapters of life.

A tool I use to assist my chaptering is my someday, maybe list, also known as my bucket list.

This list contains all the things I may do someday, maybe. Having kept this list since my late twenties, I am always amazed at the number of things I have gotten done simply for having planned to get them done. Seeing what I have gotten done always encourages me about what I can get done.

Some of the things on this list that are behind me are: 1) getting my MBA in design management from a European school, 2) visiting China and seeing the Forbidden City and the Great Wall of China,

3) being a product manager, and 4) being a published writer, speaker and professor. These are all things I could not have imagined accomplishing during a past chapter of my life, but which hoping, planning, anticipating and follow-through have seen accomplished.

Life is long enough for us to do a variety of things. Rarely are we truly locked out of what we want to do. We have to be flexible and creative in seeking ways to use the time we have to engage talents of delight in settings of appeal for purposes that love God, self, neighbor and enemy. We have to look for, and capitalize on, every element of talent, setting, and purpose that exist in our day jobs, as well as looking for ways to do the same in volunteer situations in the evenings and on weekends. It is these volunteer situations that provide opportunity for developing into areas that our day jobs do not afford us.

There is always an opportunity emerging in a next chapter of life. Daily we should balance taking best advantage of today while preparing for the someday maybe opportunities that emerge tomorrow, where tomorrow may be twenty-four hours, or years, from now.

Use this concept of chaptering to encourage yourself and to stay in action when tempted to bog down or to be discouraged by what you have not accomplished or what seems to be out of your grasp.

Delaying Gratification: Key to Success and Antidote for Procrastination

Since I am a career coach, you can imagine that the questions of attaining success and overcoming procrastination come up a lot. I would daresay that the desire to achieve success is the primary reason people approach me, and procrastination is a primary barrier to achieving success.

For years I have subscribed to the idea that procrastination can be attributed to more than laziness. We delay in starting many things because we fear we cannot do them perfectly.

Lately I have appended this impression with the thought that procrastination can also be attributed to an unwillingness to delay gratification. This came to me while recently contemplating my past readings of M. Scott Peck's, "The Road Less Travelled"., where he talks about the inability to delay gratification as a barrier to maturity, and the TED Talk presentation by Joachim de Posada, where he asserts the link between delayed gratification and life success. I recommend you Google both.

As I ponder these discussions and thoughts about my own struggle with procrastination, I realized that every time I procrastinate, I am filling that space with some activity or thought that gratifies me more than the activity or thought I should be more committed to doing *now*.

An example for me would be catching up with friends on Facebook when I should have been working on the manuscript of this very book you are holding. It would have been out years sooner had I not procrastinated so much. It is not that catching up on Facebook is bad, but that it was inappropriate at the time that I had budgeted for writing and editing. It was ultimately my unwillingness to delay my Facebook gratification that resulted in the procrastination that resulted in this book not being completed. The fact that this book is in your hands is a sign of hope.

What gratifications are you prioritizing today that are resulting in procrastination about other critical life goals you have?

Identify these gratifications and box them within certain scheduled time frames in your week. This boxing will allow you to enjoy them without them growing like weeds into other time periods during your week when you should be pursuing critical life goals like developing a new skill, cultivating a relationship, exercising, studying, volunteering, and so on. This is where your future success lies, and procrastination is the barrier. Practice delaying (not eliminating) gratification in order to stop delaying your success.

44

Volunteering as a Path to a Better or Different Career

Once a colleague asked me how he might help out more in the community, and this is what fell upon me in a stream of consciousness. This is an approach I have come to term volun-career-ing. This approach deliberately leverages volunteering as a means of developing one's resume and network towards a desired career.

1. Start with a faith-based or service community you are a member of. This is a way of investing where you can also get help when you need it.

2. Focus on problems and evils you have a passion for resolving. I do lots of career coaching because I fear the evils of poverty and meaningless work.

3. Invest money in enabling the volunteering of others. I invest in World Vision and give at my church, as this enables others.

4. Consistency over time is more important than lots of time at any given point. I have been a volunteer career coach at my church for many years now. This has resulted in my now being a certified leadership and career coach.

5. Look to serve on a board aligned with causes you want to impact in the world. It is great for contributing, learning, and networking. I serve on a local National Alliance on Mental Illness (NAMI) board, as I am interested in issues related to mental health awareness, stigma, and caregiver coping.

6. Engage family and friends to multiply the community effect, as well as to model this life habit for them. In this way, I have created skill and resume-development opportunities for my children, as they have worked in ministry in our church.

7. Volunteer in areas related to your personal and professional development to achieve multiple ends with single means. I work at social media, communications, and leadership development in my volunteering, which I take back to my day work as a more developed professional.

Clearly I am a proponent of volun-career-ing. I believe and have experienced it as a great way to: 1) build skills and experience, 2) grow my network, 3) obtain references and resume entries and 4) experiment with career options.

I am always amazed at how much my clients either neglect volunteering as a career opportunity or they volunteer and do not see it as a part of their career. Give more thought and effort to this career strategy to benefit yourself and your community.

PRACTICE: THE WISEWORKER'S PLAYGROUND

Eggs, Baskets, and Careers: A Spring Post

This post is about the Spring symbols of eggs and baskets and what they mean to your career. I love to use this analogy to help my clients appreciate what they often discount or undervalue in their resources. In this analogy, eggs are the skills, relationships and knowledge we possess, and baskets are opportunities, organizations/networks and purposes we can put our eggs into.

Most of us undercount and despise both our eggs and our baskets. We think our eggs are too small and not top quality. We think our baskets are made of the wrong material, are the wrong color, and lack the pretty bow that others' baskets possess. We refuse to contribute our eggs to baskets because either or both are displeasing to us. This displeasure is too often rooted in ours not being like others, not in the fact that they are worthless.

Another error we make is to overfavor certain eggs and baskets to the exclusion of others we possess. This error results in our having too many eggs in too few baskets, thus narrowing our options, responsiveness, development, and relationships. This leaves us more vulnerable than we need be when advancement opportunities come along or when we are invited to move on.

Let's make time to fully inventory our eggs and baskets and commit to using at least one more egg or investing in one more basket sometime soon.

P.S. And if you say that you have no time for more baskets, take the time to ask how satisfied you are with your present set of baskets and the number of eggs in them. Don't be afraid to shelve some of those baskets or to refrigerate some of those eggs in order to develop new eggs and/or baskets that will bring you more satisfaction.

PRACTICE: THE WISEWORKER'S PLAYGROUND

Giving Ourselves (and Others) a Break

In every interaction, an impression is made for better or worse. We, as human beings, are wired for the detection of the negative. We allow negative impressions to emerge and stick more easily than positive ones. We often continue to judge a person (and ourselves) in a certain fashion even after change has occurred for the better.

I find this is one of those things we are prone to doing to others and hate the most to be done to us. We overlook and discount even small improvements in others, especially if they once let us down. We correspondingly suffer because of those who won't acknowledge the small improvements we make day after day. In essence, we don't give a break and we don't get a break.

As with most interpersonal situations, it takes wisdom, judgment, skill, and risk taking to know when we should give a break and when not. The fact is that there are ways to acknowledge the improvement in others, while also protecting ourselves from their imperfection. It is usually not an all-or-nothing proposition, but it does take a deliberate and conscious effort.

The next time you are faced with the risk and threat of others' repeated offensive or dysfunctional behavior, give them a break by:

1. catching them doing better, and most importantly, acknowledging their better doing.

2. exhibiting courage to engage them in crucial conversations (I recommend the book, Crucial Conversations: Tools for Talking When Stakes Are High by Patterson) to help them toward realizations intended to effect positive change.

3. modeling (being) the change that you want to see in them, versus modeling reactive undesirable behavior.

4. giving the same amount of grace you would want to receive when you disappoint, because every day we all do.

5. proactively choosing your own response to others, rather than reactively letting others choose your response for you.

In these five practices, note that it is probably most important to do these practices to (for) ourselves, as truth be told, we need to give our own selves a break more than anyone else.

PRACTICE: THE WISEWORKER'S PLAYGROUND

47

Giving Ourselves (and Others) Credit

After giving oneself (and others) a break, I think we most neglect giving credit where some credit is almost always due. Giving credit involves acknowledging and taking stock of what we have gotten done, versus what we have not.

In my personal and coaching experience, I think that this lack of giving credit is one of the most detrimental issues we deal with when working toward goals. We often forget, or belittle, what we have accomplished as though it did not take skill, knowledge, and discipline to get to where we are. We sometimes act as though what we have was given to us without effort and skill on our part. We also think we are inadequate to get what we need in the future. A little conscious thought often proves these premises wrong.

The fact is that "We can because we have."

Our fixation on discredit discourages. Balancing discredit with credit encourages, that is, gives courage (a.k.a. heart to proact in the face of fear).

Examples of the need for giving ourselves credit are:

- when we are going for a master's degree and we discount that we somehow figured out how to get our bachelor's, so getting our master's should not be an impossibility.

- when we are going for a job offer and we discount that we got the interview and built the resume and network to get the invitation to the interview, do getting the job is a possibility.

- when we are laid off and we discount that we got the job we were laid off of and can get another.

- when we are on bad terms with others and we discount that we have built and rebuilt relationships in the past and can do it again with care, patience and persistence.

- when we really blow a task or project and we discount that we have been successfully bouncing back from such mishaps since diapers and cradles, to our ultimate benefit.

This practice of giving credit not only encourages us, but calls us to reflect on what we have accomplished. It also yields recollection of lessons learned that point to how we can better execute what is yet to be done. Adopt this practice of giving credit to encourage yourself and others.

Self-Comparison Better Than Other-Comparison (Most of the Time)

Comparison is the root of much doubt, angst and discouragement in life.

Comparison is capable of robbing us of the joy of our achievements because one can always find others who seem to have more, and to have done more. This often causes us to think that what we have and what we have achieved is less than. Very often we're using a questionable yardstick when we make such comparisons. I learned once from a mentor that (often) the best yardstick for comparison is my former self, not others.

Certainly comparison to others is useful and necessary in cases where we are engaged in direct competition. In most cases, though, we are called on to collaborate, making the best unique and relevant contribution to a situation or organization that we can with our talents, experiences, knowledge, and relationships. It is important to identify when it is most appropriate to compete versus collaborate, and when collaborating, to take pride in our own unique and relevant contribution.

This is a significantly more empowering and encouraging approach than beating ourselves up because we are not contributing exactly as others do. I feel strongly that it is better to discover and sharpen our own unique and relevant contribution and take pride in such!

I see in myself, and others, a tendency to spend too much time in negative comparison, using such as a basis for discouraging and denigrating ourselves. I think that it is imperative to better balance this with positive comparison with our former selves. This is a good basis for encouragement, pride and unique, relevant contribution. I have seen that doing this shows up how I am better today than I was yesterday, and in cases, that has resulted in my being better than my competition.

Of course, there are those days when I am not better than my former self, and forgiveness, compassion, and recommitment are in order.

PRACTICE: THE WISEWORKER'S PLAYGROUND

49

What Exhausts: The Work or the Reaction to the Work?

Whenever preparing for vacation, I find myself thinking how tired I am and how I got here. I also think about what necessitates a vacation in this knowledge work era, where we are not subject to the physical wear, tear, and hazard that were endemic of the industrial work era. It would seem that the lack of physical labor we engage in would leave us not so tired, but we all know that's wishful thinking.

As I have pondered knowledge work exhaustion in myself, it has occurred to me that the lack of physical work (like when I don't exercise three times a week) actually contributed to my exhaustion. I find that, not the work itself, but my emotional and psychological reactions to the reputational (relationship/knowledge) and project (time/money) demands, risks, and crises of my work take the most toll, manifesting as emotional, mental, and yes, physical fatigue.

I find I best manage exhaustion when I engage in the work of practicing:

- opportunity thinking;
- conscious breathing;

- present-moment openness and focus;
- forgiveness, a.k.a. letting go;
- lack of ego, a.k.a. humility; and
- passionate detachment, a.k.a. performance without attachment to the result.

I find that as I get better at these practices, my resilience and tolerance for stress, conflict, and change have increased.

All that said, and being imperfect in these practices, fatigue does accumulate, thus I benefit by staying faithful to my practice of a week off every calendar quarter.

Watching Our Work

From time to time I take inventory of my accomplishments. This is rarely an easy process, but it is insightful and encouraging.

The fact is that we do our work too much in a mindless, for-granted mode.

This leads to our losing touch with its purpose and effect in the world, which can lead to feelings of disconnection, ennui, frustration and waste. I know because I occasionally struggle with this, but also because I see this so often in my coaching, and particularly when I am asking about work histories as a part of the resume-development and interview-preparation process.

Too many are unfamiliar with, and unappreciative of, their work even as they do it. I say that work consumes entirely too much of one's life to justify this type of disconnection and mindlessness. I think methods of mindfulness, appreciative inquiry and reflective writing can stand us in good stead in this practice of watching our work. These methods help us to be present, curious and accountable in our work.

As I watch my work, it occurs to me that all my work can be nicely divided into four categories: tasks, relationships, collaborations and results. Tasks are what I do, relationships are who I know, collaboration synergizes the first two, and results are what the first three produce.

These categories are useful as a framework for watching one's work, and even for planning improvements in work from moment to moment, whether paid work, nonpaid volunteer work, housework, family work or self-work, for that matter.

I mean to suggest here that we can: 1) derive more meaning and enjoyment from our work, 2) find a greater ability to articulate the process and results of our work, and 3) purposefully develop in our work if we are more mindful and appreciatively curious about our work and what it produces in the world.

I encourage you to take advantage of this opportunity to watch your work for all the benefits that can be derived from such a practice.

COMMUNICATIONS TECHNOLOGY

The WiseWorker's Instrument
and Amplifier

Communications Technology: The WiseWorker's Instrument & Amplifier

Any of you would agree that much of our ability to have a positive impact on our work, workers or workplace comes from an ability to communicate not only well, but sufficiently broadly. The impact of communications technologies like e-mail, LinkedIn®, Twitter®, Facebook®, SlideShare®, and even iPhones® and iTunes® is phenomenal and has given more of us the ability to communicate and educate better than ever.

These communications technologies are truly the amplifiers of our perspectives, gifts, brands, stories and actions, as well as the organizer of, and connectors to, our villages. The articles in this section are about how to use these technologies in becoming a WiseWorker. Enjoy!

Facebook: Community Center and Graduate School?

By now most of us know Facebook (FB), the popular online social community, is beyond early adoption and into the mainstream as a social phenomenon. For some, it has become a lifestyle for benefit and for waste.

I have come to find FB to be an effective community center and graduate school. It's an effective community center because I spend more time with more people exchanging ideas, opinions, advice and encouragement about more topics that are relevant to my life and career than at any other time in my life. It's an effective graduate school because this community has exposed me to more people with more diverse expertise talking about more diverse views and topics at a more substantive level than since I was in my graduate school cohort. It is a true salon, and not in the get-your-hair-done sense either. Specific benefits I have derived from FB have been:

1. Richer relations and understanding of those I work, worship, and live with, as I see other dimensions of their personalities and lives through their status updates and posts. Some of the best experiences of community in my life these days is in the hourly banter of talented smart-working colleagues posting

relevant status updates, videos and articles. We share in the angst and joy of our work and empathize/encourage one another, often humorously. Indeed, every challenge is lightened when shared.

2. Connections to experts and authorities who are filling out many aspects of cultural and historic literacy that I missed along the way and whom I would not have had the occasion to meet except through friends' posts.

3. Exposure to worldviews and opinions that are rounding out my knowledge and perspective of the world and maturing my philosophy on many topics, as I take time to comment and ask probing questions on the many posts related to issues that resonate with me or that I realize I need an education on. I have at times engaged in rich debates about complex issues with friends and friends of friends that have spanned days and dozens of posts and counter-posts, leaving me at the end of an emotional, psychological, and intellectual roller coaster, and richer for the ride!

4. Exposure to organizations and causes that resonate with me, but which I did not know existed. FB not only exposes me, but then gives me the means to voice my support, connect with those working on these issues, and contribute my time, money, ideas or talent to the degree I choose.

FB, used appropriately, is a tool that can enrich one's life, enhance one's education and expand one's footprint in the society and on the planet. As usual, it's the craftsperson's skill with the tool that makes the tool useful or not, not the tool itself. I encourage you to continue to learn to be skillful users of social media tools for those purposes most resonant with you.

On Using Delicious Social Bookmarks

I have been introducing my clients to a number of the social media tools I use that help me with my WiseWorking. In this post, I am talking about social bookmarking. There are a number of services that allow you to do this. I use http://www.delicious.com, although there are other services like Diigo.com, Reddit.com, and so on. Social bookmarking is a service/technique that allows you to keep the bookmarks of websites that you now keep in the web browser bookmark lists of the various computers you use in one central space on the Internet. The benefits of social bookmarking are varied and include:

1. one central repository for all your bookmarks that are otherwise scattered across many different computers and mobile devices. You have access to them as long as you have an Internet connection and can get to www.delicious.com, where you can add new bookmarks or access those formerly bookmarked.

2. taggging, or categorization, of your bookmarks to multiple topics, making finding them much easier than in traditional bookmark lists.

3. connecting to people in the delicious network who have also bookmarked the same websites you have. This is the "social" aspect of social bookmarking, allowing you to build your network of experts and interests in a given field. It is also an opportunity to extend your own thought leadership as you post sites in your areas of expertise and comment on them.

4. easy sharing of lists of bookmarks within a topical area with your network. I typically share my delicious bookmark lists with colleagues, clients, students, readers of my articles, and so on; I construct such lists of bookmarks whenever I am doing any sort of research.

I have found this technique of social bookmarking a tremendous timesaver as it allows me to: 1) store websites I am interested in without the anxiety of forgetting them, and 2) retrieve many relevant websites I have forgotten about as they are stored under the tags that are relevant to me.

Productive bookmarking to you!

iPhone/iTunes: A Training and Development Tool?

By now, only the most die-hard of Luddites do not own an iPod or iPhone. That said, I am amazed at the number of iPod owners I question who tell me they do not use them for educational purposes. Often these individuals think of the iPod as a device for the consumption of music and overlook its uses for the consumption of educational content. I admit that most of the use of my iPod and iPhone is for the consumption of audiobooks from www.audible.com and relevant educational podcasts and college courses (in audio and video) from www.itunes.com.

I get amazed and thoughtful replies when I communicate this iPod/iPhone use behavior to others, and I am immediately asked when do I find the time to listen or watch.

The fact is that I consume iPod content consistently throughout my day like: 1) during my commute, 2) when doing chores that do not require intense concentration, 3) when falling to sleep (where the sleep timer comes in handy), 4) when washing up and dressing in the morning, 5) when working out, 6) when walking between meetings, 7) while waiting for unpunctual colleagues, 8) while sitting in the barber's chair, and so on.

As a matter of fact, I attribute much of my increased patience and quality of life to this habit, as I can always put on educational audio to soothe my annoyance with otherwise wasted time. Because I am edutained, I can better flip my perception and see downtime as a productive gift (sometimes).

Rethink the use of your iPod and iPhone as an edutainment tool to advance your personal training and development.

On Using LinkedIn

LinkedIn (LI) is a professional social network, and one of my chief career management tools. I always highly recommend it to clients and colleagues and find consistently that after signing up, they often do not have the faintest idea of how to use this tool to their advantage.

That said, I am sharing how I use LI in my daily life, with hopes it will help you:

1. **Colleague Finder**: LI has been invaluable in facilitating my reconnection with scores of old classmates, managers, mentors and colleagues. When you fully complete your profile with all the schools, companies and associations you have been a part of, the site searches its network of over 17 million users and brings you back a list of people you can choose to invite to a connection.

2. **Expert Research**: LI has been invaluable in helping me to build a network of experts in subject areas of interest. Once while doing research on the topic of narrative therapy, I was able to find an expert in South Africa who was an authority in this area. Now how else would I have found such?

3. **Opportunity Research and Recruitment**: I have found LI invaluable in connecting me with present and former company employees who have been willing to spend time with me helping me to understand industries, companies and partnership situations. You would be surprised who will be interested in helping you out when you make a proposal for assistance. LI's Jobs section, allows one to find available jobs and candidates and to connect with the hiring manager or potential candidate.

4. **Topical Research**: LI's Groups & wall have been great for putting questions to the community. I have used it to get insight into decisions I have to make, to survey strategies and tactics being deployed in the marketplace, to find job candidates, and so on. In addition to asking, I have also answered questions in my areas of expertise as a way of contributing to the community and building my reputation and expertise. As you know, nothing teaches like teaching, and certainly answering community questions helps in this regard.

5. **Contact List**: Though I keep contact lists in Outlook, I have found LI to be a handy tool for searching for, and finding, particular groups of contacts based on keywords, a dimension that is lost in elsewhere where people's profiles are not existent.

6. **Business Card and Resume**: Because my profile is fully populated, I find that increasingly when I meet new people, I refer them to my LI profile and ask them to send me a connection as this is both my business card and resume. This is also a great strategy for building connections.

7. **Recommendations**: This is a great LI feature that allows former managers, colleagues, and reports to write a recommendation related to their impressions of you and your performance. Yes, you get to proof and approve the written recommendations before they are posted. I have actually had search professionals approach me asking for candidate recommendations with the stipulation that they must be LI members with LI recommendations. I assume they use these as a screening mechanism. I highly recommend you write recommendations for people you think are extraordinary, and watch how the law of reciprocity works for you.

On Using Twitter

Twitter, on which one tweets, is a social media service based on the premise of microblogging, where people communicate in 140-character blurbs to their followers.

Now when most professionals hear this premise, their immediate response is, "I do not have time or interest in letting others know what I am doing all day long," and I agreed until I started using the service. I was informed, and subsequently found, that while most of the tweets on Twitter are rather mundane, there are tweeters out there, who can be found using Twitter's keyword search, who are tweeting information in knowledge areas that are relevant to both my professional and personal life. There are also some tweeters I follow whose lives are humorous and entertaining by degrees.

I have found the use of this service beneficial as a running news feed. It's like a newspaper where I customize the stories and only get the headlines. Most headlines have a link to body copy I can click to if I choose. For instance, the other day, I received insight into the blow-by-blow proceedings of a health-care conference from a tweeter I follow, complete with relevant URL links.

On the flip side, I have found that my own tweeting has benefited me in: 1) allowing me to compile a running diary of my own activities, insights, and perceptions throughout the day; 2) contributing to the community of individuals who are following me, as they are interested in the same things I am and 3) expanding my network beyond what I have gathered on the other social media services I already use.

For some, this will be yet another overwhelming item they have to attend to in their busy day, and this crowd should stay away, but for those who want to offer knowledge to a community of interest as well as serendipitously gain the same, I recommend Twitter.

My Unintended Social Media Education Strategy

A connection on LinkedIn asked me how I went about managing my presence in social communities. I had not really given this much thought until I settled down to answer this question.

In past chapters you have heard me allude to social media as my graduate school, community center, and training and development tool, and this value continues to grow for me as I both give and receive value in these venues. I find that I am a natural teacher and student. As such, I am gratified to use social media as an extended and ongoing university, where I can exercise this role within a broader community.

Below is the reply I wrote to my inquiring LinkedIn connection. It is roundabout, but I hope it helps you in some way as you too think about how you can leverage social media for your own purposes, whether university, employment office, corner (like in the old neighborhood) where you enjoyed good times with friends, and so on.

My social media methods include:

1. Blogging on www.wiseworking.com, facebook.com, Google+ and twitter.com about topics of meaningful working and careering, social media, healthcare marketing, and so on, all topics I am passionate about.

2. Keeping and sharing my Delicious (and now Diigo.com) bookmark links (see chapter 52, "On Using Delicious Social Bookmarks") of just about everything I am researching online. 3. Keeping status updates in Facebook, LinkedIn, and Twitter (which are fed from HootSuite.com) with just about everything professionally beneficial I am thinking or researching.

3. Joining relevant communities in LinkedIn, Facebook, Google+ and other relevant social communities online, and keeping these lists as Delicious bookmark lists by interest area so I can find them easily.

4. Making relevant counter comments with resource links in LinkedIn, Facebook, Twitter, LinkedIn and using my Diigo bookmarks as a way of being able to very quickly find these resources.

5. Posting relevant slide and video content on my SlideShare and YouTube channels, which I then feature as blog posts.

6. Keeping a collection of all my portfolio pieces at https://www.diigo.com/user/cadelarge/cadelarge_portfolio, for easy reference and sharing.

I know this is a lot. Understand that I do all this rather unconsciously in the flow of my daily work and play, so I would caution you against feeling pressure to do the same. Don't do it because it's cool but because it benefits you. And even if you do not do this, by all means connect to people who do, and benefit from their activities in posting content of beneficial interest to you.

RESULTS

The WiseWorker's Legacy

Results: The Wiseworker's Legacy

A great reward of work is its results, both in the journey of the process and the destination of the goal. Indeed, the result of our work is our legacy and a prime element of our personal brand. In both the short and long term, the results we produce are, aside from relationships, all we can leave in the world at our departure. These following chapters are about results, how to identify them, leverage them, and be proud of them.

In this final section, we examine failure as a path to success, the connections between the labor of work and that of childbirth, the importance of managing our margin and time well, of not giving up too soon in the pursuit of our legacy, and of using our reasons, a.k.a. excuses, to our best advantage.

Enjoy!

Failing To(ward) Success

For most of my life, I have struggled with a fear of failure. I think I, and most people I know, have been robbed of more opportunity by this fear than by anyone or anything else in our lives.

The fact is that the thing we fear, failure, is the thing we are doing on an ongoing basis all our lives. Every minute of every day I am: 1) attempting something, 2) not getting the result I wanted, and 3) applying what I have learned from the prior attempt to get closer to the result I want. I am in essence failing, and as a result, succeeding. I am failing to(ward) success, and in doing so, not failing to succeed.

I am failing to success in the most insignificant things, like rewriting my signature after I have made a mistake, to more significant tasks like reworking an analysis whose assumptions have been discounted by my management, to really big disasters like retaking a class that I have failed in school. What is common about these examples is that they are not really failures as much as learning in process.

The failure is not in failing to get the result I wanted, but in not learning and adapting in order to get the result I wanted. In this, we see that we are always failing to(ward) success if we are persisting in applying our learnings through practice.

This thought gives me confidence and perspective, as it relates to the things I plan to accomplish. Indeed, there is no failure, only learning. Remember that the next time you want to quit, not try again, or bail out when perceiving that you have failed.

Failure Needs No Plan

In the book *Think and Grow Rich*, Napoleon Hill talks about the idea that "failure needs no plan." This paradox has always intrigued me. It single-handedly expresses two meanings. The first is that one need not plan to fail, as failure is the default occurrence when one does not plan. The second is that failure does not need us to have a plan in order to occur. One might say further that, "Failure and the lack of a plan tend to go hand in hand." (Yes, I did intend to rhyme there.)

While planning does not guarantee success, it results in a higher probability of such. I believe that even a failed plan yields more learning (and a corresponding greater chance of future success) than a failure that occurred as a result of no planning at all.

In my coaching, as well as in my own life, I see the stark manifestation of this saying on a regular basis. After negative thinking and a lack of persistence and patience, the lack of a plan is probably the greatest barrier to the achievement of our potential.

For this reason, we should be committed to planning, as at best, it yields success, and at worst, learning. Below are a few ponder points to use as you plan for your own success:

1. Remember that every plan must account for barriers and setbacks. Factor them in and do not be shocked when they occur.

2. Consider how easy it is to be more committed to others' plans than to your own. Be at least as true to yourself as to others and seek synergy between your plans and those of the important and significant others in your life.

3. Prepare plans B, C, and so on, as few plan A's execute as originally planned.

4. In planning, discipline yourself to enjoy the process of planning and execution as much as the destination. The destination is in the uncertain future, whereas the execution is always in the present moment. When you practice the disciplines of staying present and passionate detachment, you get a reward every moment, as well as the reward of satisfaction with the outcome at the destination. "Chop wood, carry water," for those of you familiar with this Zen maxim.

5. Remember that an average plan excellently executed is better than an excellent plan poorly executed or not executed at all.

The Pain (and Satisfaction) of Labor

I find that whenever I experience restlessness, fatigue, frustration, impatience, or any number of other unpleasant emotions or attitudes related to my work, it helps when I zoom out to reconnect with the result I am working to bring into the world.

I have to remember that bringing my work to fruition is much like bringing a child into the world. It requires labor, which is consistent with what they call it, eh? As with childbirth, the labor is difficult, but what joy and satisfaction as soon as the child (the result) is brought into being. The sweat, pain, and persistence it takes are just part of the process, not unusual, and to be expected. Keeping our eyes on the anticipated results helps a lot in the process.

To take this analogy a step further, I encourage us all to examine and appreciate the results (the children) of our labor on a regular basis. Too often we are quick to denigrate and not appreciate the results of our work. Taking solace in what we are producing, especially on tough days, gives us the persistence, patience, and other necessary emotions and attitudes to stay with it until we get the end we desire.

Wisely Investing Our Own Profit (Margin)

Regularly, I read a book called *The Daily Drucker*, a collection of excerpts from books by the great management philosopher Peter F. Drucker. A recent excerpt talked about the topic of profit and how profit is the cost of business that provides the opportunity for innovation and the development of competencies that allow an organization to adapt to and shape change.

While reading, it occurred to me that this idea regarding the purpose and application of profit (or margin) is as applicable to organisms as to organizations. It is especially critical as we see the decline of long-term employment in corporate organizations.

The fact is that we all have the opportunity to make and invest the profit (or margin) in our lives in terms of emotional and physical energy, time, and money.

If you are one who is not taking advantage of this opportunity, I highly recommend the book, *Margin,* by Richard A. Swenson, MD. Once we have begun to manage our personal profit margin, like we are so good at doing for our businesses, we then have to consider how to invest it. The options are many and there are probably more wasteful ways of investing than beneficial, but if we want to be as good personal managers as organizational, we have to take stock of how we are investing and assure that the investment of our spare energy, time, and money is strategic (creating a competitive advantage) and balanced.

So often in my managing and coaching, I hear people say that they have no energy, time or money margin. As I hear this, I wonder if this is because they really have no margin or because they are in need of more skillful management of the margin that is available to them. As a business does not profit without skillful management and focus, neither do we.

The fact is that the ways in which we are good today may someday be obsolete and we must continually look to upskill and reskill to shape and adapt advantageously (strategically) to inevitable change. Joseph Schumpeter, the famous twentieth-century economist and political scientist, coined the phrase *creative destruction* as a useful activity of management that purposes to destroy the present in lieu of a better future before someone else does. This is what I am talking about when I allude to the opportunity of shaping change.

I want to suggest that the primary change that is shapable is in ourselves and that the resource for doing that is our margin of energy, time, and money.

I know that I must be continually careful to assure that I do not waste too much of my spare energy, time and money on investments that do not: 1) regenerate future energy, time, and money; 2) feed my values, passions, and interests; and 3) sharpen my saw, as Stephen Covey would say.

Such consistent investing results in:

1. More energy, (perceived) time, and money.
2. Greater contribution of value to those I serve in every area of my life.
3. Heightened innovation and creativity in my work and service.
4. Greater awareness and resilience to shape and adapt to change.
5. Increased footprint of my influence and impact on the communities I belong to.

So let's give thought to how we use our profit margin so that our strategic and balanced investment of this margin will benefit ourselves and our community.

Time: What Are You Making with Yours?

"I don't have time" is quickly becoming one of the great mantras (and excuses) of this present age.

The fact that there is a touch of truth in every lie is definitely the case here. The truth is that we have time and we don't. The lie is in why this is the case. We say that we don't have time (because of factors outside of us in our environment), and that is partially true because time is what we make more than what we have.

We have all been given the same 168 hours per week, something we can only say about time as we are all given different amounts of money, talent, relationships, knowledge, and so on. This equality is one of the reasons time is the most important resource we have, and what makes what we make with time a most critical activity of life.

The fact is that everything we have, from how we think to our possessions, to our careers, to our relationships, we make with the time we have been given. This then obviously begs the question of "What are we making with our time?"

This question is first one of priority. When we say we do not have time for something, we are really saying it is not a priority, and often this is justified, as most of us are pursuing too many priorities to begin with.

I began to learn this lesson on September 11, 2001, when the events of that morning stopped me dead to refocus in order to make time for informing myself about the events of that day and to see about my community. It was so striking to me how quickly so many important things could become not so important. I learned that for the rest of my life, I have a choice to make time for what is important to me because we only ever have time for what we make time for.

The second issue is one of focus. It is difficult to maintain focus on what is important in the midst of all the urgent and unimportant things that come up continually in life.

It is too easy to use time to attend to the urgent and unimportant while neglecting the making of those memories, relationships, education and results that are truly important to us. A critical factor in making what's important with the time we are given is learning to say no to the urgent and unimportant, and if this is a challenge for you, see chapter 41, "No: The New Yes."

Take time today to consider how you prioritize and focus, and what you make with your time.

Are you making important results, relationships, memories, people, objects, and so on with your time, or are you making procrastination, worry, poor plans that lead to urgent emergencies, focus on unimportant issues?

As we take more responsibility for making time for what's important, and making what's important with that time we are given, we can move from a posture of "I do not have time" to "I make time for what is truly important to me."

Now isn't that a more powerful way to approach life?

Don't Call the Game Before It's Over

I want to encourage you to play the game until it's over, and not to call it lost before it is over.

This is something I see too often in my coaching. People who bail out of an opportunity psychologically and emotionally before they do thorough research and get advice. People who won't apply for a job because they are not 100 percent qualified (when no one ever is). People who won't stay focused through multiple interviews because they anticipate that they will not get an offer. People who lose raises, better assignments and promotions because they will not do research and lobby for the opportunity.

I like to advise these individuals to not to call the game before it's over. So many of life's opportunities are lost due to lack of discipline and persistence and overuse of negative speculation.

I am the first to admit that even I do not always take the advice I am giving here. I will further admit that some games do need to be called before over in order to put that time and energy into other games that are more important and that constitute a better chance of winning.

The fact is that you can only play so many games simultaneously well, and that you cannot win every game. That said, I believe we can win more than we do with more emotional, psychological, and relational discipline and persistence and less negative speculation.

Over time, as I have grown and matured, I have become relatively better at playing through to the end of the game. Below I share a number of devices that help me when I am up against my own fatigue in the middle, or even at the beginning, of a game:

1. **Emotional mindfulness is needed,** as most bailing out happens first at an emotional level, which affects our thinking and then our actions. Being aware of my emotional state at the time I bail out helps me to better diagnose what is going on and to recommit. I have to continually remind myself that feelings are not facts.

2. **Regaining perspective by testing reality with others** is a critical use of my mentors and colleagues. I can be prone to being myopic and overwhelmed at times, losing both the big picture and long-term perspective relative to my goals. Running situations by trusted advisors to test my view of reality is a big help that helps me to remember why I am really playing the game and why I need to stay committed to finishing it.

3. **Recommitment to love and fearlessness is important** because we are always operating from one of these positions or its opposite. Fear is negative, selfish and exhausting. Love is positive, service-oriented, and energizing. When I am ready to bail out for no good reason, I check to see if I have disconnected from love and plugged into fear. I know that I always have a choice to reverse this connection.

4. **Being patient and persistent,** as every game is longer and takes more effort to win than initially envisioned. With this in mind, I learn not to be surprised or demoralized when this fact asserts itself.

5. **Researching the game** I am playing, its players and rules, so that I can get better at it, knowing that no one is good at any game at the beginning but anyone can become expert with good observation and practice. This occurs through the methods of reading, case studies, networking, role-playing, shadowing, and so on.

6. **Accessing the resource needed to finish the game** is critical, as we often find that we do not know all the resources we need when we start playing. This is part of research and learning, not an excuse for bailing out. As we learn, we adapt to get those resources we find we need, whether they be education, experience, time, relationships, or even money. I intentionally put money last, because we often think it most important, when in fact it is least important of the aforementioned resources.

7. **Overcoming the barriers to winning,** as this is the essential element that makes a game a game. This can in fact be the most satisfying element of playing any game. It is critical to understand and anticipate internal and external barriers to winning, and to plan for how we will overcome them.

So, let's look at the important games we have been called to, meditate on the methods mentioned above, and recommit to winning those games.

How You Use Your Reasons Determines Whether You Get Results

An axiom I picked up years ago when I went through the Landmark Forum is that "In life, you always get one of two things, either a result you want, or a reason for why you did not get the result you wanted." This has always stayed with me.

One way of looking at this axiom is that excuses and results are always options we choose and that to befriend one is to make an enemy of the other.

Looking deeper, the fact is that sometimes all you have are reasons (as none of us succeed all the time). The point to be taken from this is related to how we use our reasons.

Do we use them as excuses, or as learning that moves us closer to the results we are aiming for?

When you consider those instances when you have not gotten the results you wanted, what have you been most prone to do with the resulting reasons? Have you used them as excuses or as learnings? The way to know that you are doing the latter is if you stay in action toward your desired results, getting smarter and closer all the time.

Take time today to consider what you are doing with your reasons, especially in those areas of your life where you are most dissatisfied

Results: The Wiseworker's Legacy

with your results. You will find that you need to make changes based on your learning. Of course, if you are not interested in changing, you will likely just continue to use your reasons as excuses.

Either way, you will have your results or your reasons.

Epilogue

Thank you for taking the time to read this collection of insights related to wise working. These writings have been a labor of love and passion for me over a number of years, fueled by my desire to see more wise working in our organizations and networks for the good of both our individual and societal health.

Life is too short, health and relations too fragile, and work too life-consuming for us not to look closely and often at how wisely we are going about it. I am convinced and have witnessed that when we do not, we harm ourselves, our families, and society.

About WiseWorking Leadership and Career Coaching

Wise Working delivers insights & insightful engagements on meaningful careers and working via its blog, www.wiseworking.com, workshops, and coaching. Working well and constructing a successful career & work life takes wisdom and persistent practice, and we are passionate about assisting careerists and leaders in developing both.

The **WiseWorking.com blog** is where we periodically jot down our latest musings, which eventually end up in our books and workshops.

The **WiseWorking Workshops** (say that ten times) are offered to allow our clients to work with the processes we recommend. The added advantage of this approach is that clients get to do so in a community setting, where they can gain support from the stories, experience, and input of others.

WiseWorking Coaching is the coaching service we provide that allows our clients to work on specific personal career, work and leadership challenges.

We can be reached at Craig@WiseWorking.com, the twitter handle, @wiseworking and www.WiseWorking.com.

Bibliography

Allen, David. *Getting Things Done: The Art of Stress-Free Productivity.* New York: Viking, 2001.

Bolles, Richard Nelson. *What Color is Your Parachute?, 2012.* 40th anniversary ed., rev. ed. Berkeley, CA: Ten Speed Press, 2012.

Brandon, Rick, and Marty Seldman. *Survival of the Savvy: High-integrity Political Tactics for Career and Company Success.* New York: Free Press, 2004.

Burroughs, John. *Zen Page-a-day Calendar.* New York: Workman Publishing Group, 2013.

Carlson, Richard. *Don't Sweat the Small Stuff—and it's All Small Stuff: Simple Ways to Keep the Little Things From Taking Over Your Life.* New York: Hyperion, 1997.

Coelho, Paulo. *The Alchemist.* San Francisco: HarperSanFrancisco, 1993.

Covey, Stephen R.. *The Seven Habits of Highly Effective People: Restoring the Character Ethic.* New York: Simon and Schuster, 1989.

Drucker, Peter F., and Joseph A. Maciariello. *The Daily Drucker: 366 Days of Insight and Motivation for Getting the Right Things Done.* New York: HarperBusiness, 2004.

Flickstein, Matthew. *The Meditator's Workbook: a Journey to the Center.* Boston: Wisdom Publications, 2009.

Fronsdal, Gil. *Right Livelyhood.* Audio Dharma.com, 2012.

Kise, Jane A. G., David Stark, and Sandra Krebs Hirsh. *Lifekeys: Discovering Who You Are, Why You're Here, What You Do Best.* Minneapolis, Minn.: Bethany House Publishers, 1996.

Koestenbaum, Peter, and Peter Block. *Freedom and Accountability at Work: Applying Philosophical Insight to the Real World.* San Francisco: Jossey-Bass/Pfeiffer, 2001.

Loehr, James E., and Tony Schwartz. *The Power of Full Engagement: Managing Energy, Not Time, Is the Key to High Performance and Personal Renewal.* New York: Free Press, 2003.

Moore, Thomas. *Thomas Moore on Meaningful Work.* Louisville: Sound True, Inc., 1999.

McCreadie, Karen, and Napoleon Hill. *Napoleon Hill's Think and Grow Rich a 52 Brilliant Ideas Interpretation.* Oxford: Infinite Ideas, 2008.

Patterson, Kerry. *Crucial Conversations: Tools for Talking When Stakes Are High.* New York: McGraw-Hill, 2002.

Peck, M. Scott. *The Road Less Traveled: A New Psychology of Love, Traditional Values, and Spiritual Growth.* New York: Simon and Schuster, 1978.

Posada, Joachim de. "Joachim de Posada: Don't eat the Marshmallows." Filmed February 2009. TED video, 5:58. Posted February 2009.http://www.ted.com/talks/joachim_de_posada_says_don_t_eat_the_marshmallow_yet

Ruiz, Miguel. *The Four Agreements: A Practical Guide to Personal Freedom*. San Rafael, Calif.: Amber-Allen Pub.:, 1997.

Swenson, Richard A. *Margin: Restoring Emotional, Physical, Financial, and Time Reserves to Overloaded Lives*. Colorado Springs, Colo.: NavPress, 1992.

Zander, Rosamund Stone, and Benjamin Zander. *The Art of Possibility*. Boston, Mass.: Harvard Business School Press, 2000.

Colophon

COVER DESIGN BY
George Allen of Design|Strategy|Research|Inc., Victoria, B.C., Canada
Artwork created using Adobe InDesign v5.5
Main title type is ITC Berkeley Oldstyle
Secondary title set in Copperplate
Back cover copy set in Myriad Pro
Cover color is Pantone blue 072 with accents of Pantone gold 871

INTERIOR DESIGN BY
Bobbi Benson of Wild Ginger Press
Artwork created using Adobe InDesign CS6
Body type set in ITC Galliard
Secondary type set in Copperplate

Printed in paper and ebook versions by Balboa Press

www.ingramcontent.com/pod-product-compliance
Lightning Source LLC
Chambersburg PA
CBHW032009170526
45157CB00002B/619